The Musings
of a
Retired Policeman

To Barry
Warmest Best Wishes
Alan

ALAN HALE
March 2023

The Musings

of a

Retired Policeman

A different world then
Arguably a better world

ALAN HALE

PC 2413 of the Avon and Somerset Constabulary 1966–1997
Police Long Service and Good Conduct Medal

THE CHOIR PRESS

First published in the United Kingdom in 2023 by
The Choir Press

ISBN: 978-1-78963-344-3

Front cover: With kind permission of Mirrorpix

Contents

The Reason

This book has been a work in progress for a couple of decades and was inspired by a number of factors. For over twenty years I have being presenting talks to various group: initially the Women's Institute (WI) but also other groups as my name spread throughout the network that is ladies' groups and indeed, latterly, men's or mixed groups. At the second performance I was asked whether I had written everything down. When my answer was no, I was told quite firmly by a lady that I should because it was history. This was the first factor.

The second factor came with the arrival of my wonderful grandchildren. It was time I made this record for them, and if in the telling of it others enjoy the story, then I shall be pleased.

The recollections you find further on may not be complete and may not necessarily be compiled in chronological order, nor in the form of chapters! The word 'random' comes to mind, but hopefully of interest anyway. So let's get started.

Dedication

This story has to be dedicated to my family, to my wife, Jane, 'the girl with the inky legs', who has been my support since I was 16. She gave me two wonderful daughters, Sarah and Clare, who in turn have given me five wonderful grandchildren (below) – in order of appearance, Corey, Mitchell, Leah, Molly and Harry – not forgetting step-grandchildren, Ryan and Sami. As I complete this in early 2022, Corey is 24 and the others go down a year at a time.

Grandchildren from left to right: Corey, Mitchell, Leah, Molly and Harry

Acknowledgement

This book has been a long time in the writing and it would not be here at all had it not been for the prompting of a lady at a WI meeting over twenty years ago, so a thank you to her.

A big thank you to all of the fine people who have played a part in my life's journey, both within the police service and without in 'civvy street'. It has been a privilege to have worked with you and for you.

A special mention to my family, who have made my life worthwhile and given me a great deal of love and pleasure.

Thank you to Hugo Pike OBE for his kindness in agreeing to write the foreword. It was much appreciated.

Finally, a thank you to Rachel at The Choir Press for her help and direction and to Naomi Music, who edited this book, putting right the matters I had got wrong.

Best wishes to you all,

Alan

Foreword

Alan and I served our local communities as police officers, initially in the Bristol Constabulary and, from 1974, in the Avon and Somerset force. Our careers took different paths, only coming together occasionally through his thirty-one years.

These 'musings' amply illustrate the job as it was – in what he and I would argue were 'the best years' – during relatively peaceful times and occasionally when community policing had to be put on hold while the genial 'bobby on the beat' had to become part of that 'thin blue line' standing between the mob and the rest of society, a mob intent on challenging the rule of law and determined to impose its will on the peaceful majority.

Alan performed his duties without fear or favour and in the best traditions of the civilian-style system of British policing at a time when it was the envy of the world. The 'musings' contain a large number of examples of how he balanced the need to enforce the law when necessary with taking a more relaxed approach when appropriate.

His commitment to the service shines right through his adult life, embracing his approach to front-line policing and his many and varied roles outside work. Members of his communities had nothing to fear from Alan and a great deal to be thankful for throughout his years of service.

Although primarily written for members of his own family, Alan's 'musings' will also interest others who lived through the same times and shared some of his experiences.

Hugo Pike OBE
Formerly PC 128 C, Bristol Constabulary, and latterly Assistant Chief Constable, Avon and Somerset Constabulary.

Introduction

The purpose of this story is to set down my life in print, mainly for the benefit of my daughters and more importantly for my grandchildren, and also for you, dear reader. I had no written record of my family history, and my parents have now passed on, so there is little I can record. I do not want my children, and indeed my grandchildren, to be in that position. I am nobody special, but perhaps I am to them, and who knows when we will not wake up! As I moved into my fifties (now completing it in my seventies), nostalgia, together with a degree of melancholy, sets in. Here was I, now suddenly the oldest male in our arm of the family. I lost my mother a year and a day after my father figure (my father-in-law, Victor Neal), and my own dad died in 1968.

However, the loss was followed by the arrival of grandchildren, and with it such committed love for them as I would not have believed. The melancholy, sadness and tears come from knowing the obvious: that I will not be able to spend all of their life with them watching them grow and hopefully, God willing, have a wonderful life. My main ambition now is to live long enough to see them all wed, or at least settled in life, and who knows, perhaps enjoy some great-grandchildren.

Perhaps it is this time of life that we remember what we were, knowing that the excitement and future is now much less than it was because the majority of life is behind us. It is remembering small things from the past, such as on a journey up the M4 noticing the large aerial erected near the Membury Services. It was searching for the first sight of that aerial that helped keep Sarah and Clare occupied when they were young and we were off to visit Jane's dad and June, his wife (Jane's stepmum) in London. It was our halfway stage and toilet stop.

Memories are so valuable; I always say that if the house were on fire, I would have to make valiant efforts to save the photographs that are contained in some two dozen or more albums, and nowadays also the stand-alone hard disc.

My police service was something that came about by chance; it was not the fulfilment of a childhood ambition but it gave me a paid hobby for thirty-one years and hopefully made my parents proud of me. It was a career full of excitement, and a bit of utter fear on three or four occasions. Where else do they pay you to ride a horse, drive high-powered cars and ride large motorcycles? Rushing through the traffic with sirens and blue lights going has to be one of the ultimate buzzes.

Retirement from the police service gave me an opportunity to explore other walks of life; having been in the police service for thirty-three years, including an initial two years in the cadet corps, I then had three further jobs in five years. Now, in full retirement, I have amassed five jobs in total after the police. Yes, there is life after the police force; if you look for it, that is.

Childhood and Family

Early Years

My first day on this earth came on 1 June 1947, thanks to my parents, Clifford Francis and Ethel Amena Hale; my first granddaughter, Leah, has now been given Amena as her middle name. My father was a telephone engineer with Reliance Telephones in Lawford's Gate, Bristol, and it was in the city and county of Bristol that we lived – 139 City Road, St Pauls, was home.

Me (age unknown).

City Road, and indeed St Pauls, was at that time a very nice area, but an area that had in fact been even grander at one time. Our house, which was rented, was an end of terrace next to St Barnabas School (now the Malcolm X Community Centre). Next door to us were Mr and Mrs Barrett, a lovely couple who often took me to the cinema at the Metropole in Sussex Place, just down the road, later destroyed in the St Pauls riots.

Arranged over four levels, the house provided enough accommodation for my parents, my grandparents on my mum's side, Sydney Walter and Amina 'Minny' Hall, and me. At times the top floor was let out to others, presumably to help with the rent.

The basement provided the kitchen and the room where we ate, while at the rear was the coal house, serviced by a chute that was accessed on the front path. A set of steps took you down to the basement door at the front of the house, from where you could enter the rear garden. In that basement room, I recollect that we had an open fire, and we spent much time there.

The front garden was just a level hard surface where as a toddler I spent many happy hours on my rocking horse. From the front garden you climbed a short flight of steps to the front door. This led through a passageway, firstly to the front living room, which was kept tidy and hardly used – it was really Nan and Gramps's room, I believe – then at the back of the house was the main living room, where we sat of an evening and listened to Rediffusion cable wireless. One of my favourite programmes was *Journey into Space*. We did not have a TV at that time; I think we got one during the mid-1950s.

There was a toilet on the half-landing between the living room level and the first floor, a toilet that never knew toilet paper, as I remember, but torn up newspaper did the job. There were two bedrooms on the first floor; my parents and I used the rear room, while my grandparents used the front. On the top floor there were three rooms, and these were the ones that were sublet. There was no bathroom. I well remember that the bedroom had lino on the floor, which in the cold weather was like stepping onto a block of ice. Ice was also well present on the windows, internally, on very cold mornings.

It was a happy childhood, as I recall, and while City Road is now a very busy route, back then, despite being a young age, playing out on the pavement was safe. Collecting discarded bus tickets from the pavement and gutter was one interest, and if my friends and I wandered up the road towards the city centre, we would reach a bomb site on the corner of Brigstocke Road, where we were able to play among the remains of a house that had clearly got in the way of a German bomb. The site was also a mass of buddleia, and in the summer the attendant butterflies. On the opposite side of the road was the Docklands Settlement.

Sadly, the bomb site was not the last site to suffer an explosion in the neighbourhood. I was in our back sitting room one morning, with my mum, when there was an almighty explosion, such that the rear windows rattled in their frames. This turned out to be an explosion at the garage at the top of Dalrymple Road, junction of Ashley Road, less than a quarter of a mile from us in a straight line. An underground petrol tank had exploded, killing nine people. A further two died from their injuries later. I imagine that that blast must have been doubly frightening for Mum, as no doubt she would have experienced the bombing of Bristol during the Second World War, and that sudden massive explosion must have brought it all back.

On Saturday, 24 November 1951, a petrol tanker was discharging a delivery to the M & M Motor Mart when the blast occurred, destroying the building and the two flats above it. Flying glass and debris and burning fuel killed eleven and injured many others, including two small boys who had been admiring motorcycles in the garage window at the time. The force of the blast damaged surrounding buildings and shattered windows up to a quarter of a mile away. Blazing petrol ran down the gutters and it took firemen two hours to get the blaze under control. They would spend the weekend working around the clock by floodlights to find all the dead.

Dalrymple Road was the scene of one of my early successes. It was there that I learnt to ride a two-wheel pedal cycle, built by the older brother of one of my friends.

My grandparents on my mum's side had started life as country folk. Initially, Sydney had been a gamekeeper at Powderham Castle in Devon and had later moved to just outside Weston-super-Mare, living in a cottage near Loxton, again as a gamekeeper. They were blessed with three sons and a daughter, my mother. Sadly, only one of her brothers was still alive when I came into the world. Uncle Arthur survived and played a big part in my life, spending almost every Sunday lunchtime with us. He

My mum with Sydney and Amina, my maternal grandparents, at Loxton. I believe Uncle Arthur is on the right but sadly cannot identify the two uncles I never knew. Below is Uncle Arthur.

took me out in his delivery van at times and let us holiday in his caravan at Sand Bay, near Weston. When he died he left me his minivan, which was very welcome at the time, with a young family and little spare money to buy vehicles.

From gamekeeping, Sydney and Amina moved to the Bath Arms at Cheddar and were 'mine host' there for a time before moving to Bristol to run the Black Swan in Eastville. They had retired when I came along, and sadly I never knew my grandfather very well because he died at home when I was about 4. I do remember, however, the lady across the road coming over to help wash his body, and then being taken by my mum into the best-kept front room to say goodnight to Granddad as he lay in his coffin. It is sad that that would not happen today. The through lounge has a lot to answer for!

This is me and my blonde curls with Nan and Gramps Hall
(my mother's parents).

Dad's parents lived in Kensington Road, St George, next door to his brother, Harold, and their two sons, Roy and Brian. Frank George and Emily Roseena Hale (my paternal grandparents) had lived in St George for most if not all of their lives. They had moved into the house following their retirement from a general store they had run for forty years, and during those forty years, they had never taken a holiday. Frank had started his working life as a bootmaker, making boots, mainly for the army – an army he became part of during the First World War. He served in the catering corps but at the front line. When he returned from the war, he went back to the boot industry, but it had started to run down, so it was then that they took the shop.

During this time, Frank put his skills as a confectioner to good use and made all manner of cakes from the shop, for weddings, birthdays, and also Christmas puddings. Grampy Hale made the wedding cakes for Harold's two sons and for my wedding in 1968.

They both lived to the wonderful age of 94. All the time I knew him he was nicknamed 'Major', which was probably due to his immaculate turnout, his very upright stance and his handlebar moustache – not a big one, but very smart.

At the age of 5 I started at St Barnabas School, just next door. Very handy; I was never late. Schooldays were fun. I became a Cub, again at the school, and remember carrying the flag for a church parade. Another memory is of the first black child to attend St Barnabas School. He was the start of the second-generation immigrants and I am sure he suffered some bullying because of his obvious differences. Thankfully, things are different now. I believe, and certainly hope, that, despite the 'race-relations industry' and the Black Lives Matter movement, society is much more multicultural. My eldest grandchild, Corey, when young, had a friend of mixed race and yet Corey has never to my knowledge mentioned or questioned his skin colour – perhaps the innocence of a 4-year-old, but they can be equally blunt and open. As I continue to put this together, Corey is now in his twenty-fourth year and is as tall as I am.

Dad had a break from the telephone business at one stage, when he went to Avonmouth Docks as a 'checker'. I do not think that lasted very long and he went back to Reliance, which at some point, I believe, became GEC. I could not really see my dad as someone happily working on the dockside. A memorable thing about my dad was his beautiful handwriting, probably the reason I admire calligraphy and try to do a bit myself.

When I was 7 my brother John Richard was born. A birthday present perhaps, as he too arrived on 1 June, in 1954, a feat to be repeated just short of half a century later when my daughter Sarah gave birth to Harry a year to the day after Molly. However, Sarah topped it by having them both delivered in the back of the ambulance taking her to the hospital. I do not think that Sarah or Clare ever experienced a long period of labour.

What I did not know when John was born was that my mum had suffered something like four miscarriages during those seven years. Anyway, I was no longer an only child.

Perhaps it was John's arrival that set the wheels in motion to find suitable accommodation so my parents did not have to share their bedroom with two children. I recall in 1957 going with my dad to look at some council houses. Two were on offer in different estates in Bristol. Although I visited them both, I did not get to look at the one in Keynsham – 64 Coronation Avenue – that we eventually moved into. At that time, as part of the process, my father had to travel to Keynsham to be interviewed by the town clerk to see whether he was a suitable person to be given a house there. Thankfully, he was. I cannot help but wonder how my life might have been different, through peer pressure, had we gone to a Bristol estate. Would I have ended up on the other side of the police riot shield? I would like to think not, because my parents, while having very little, gave me a very good start in life, and I believe that their values would have won through.

So, we were to leave Bristol and St Barnabas School behind us . . . my first school, the school that had taken me as part of its party to sing at the Colston Hall in the All-Bristol School Choir; the main memory of that was at the rehearsal, when Pamela whatshername wet herself all over the floor of the choir stalls. I had also been picked to play in the newly formed school football team but moved before the first match. I did volunteer to catch a bus back and play in the first game but that offer was not taken up! The school never had a playing field, so we went to Eastville Park to play. I also remember the head teacher hitting me across the back of the legs with a ruler for some reason. Funnily enough, it did not mentally scar me for life; more, perhaps, it prepared me for life. Perhaps in these soft liberal times there is a lesson to be learnt from that. The term 'snowflake' is now much in use regarding the resilience, or lack, of some nowadays.

It was at City Road that my nan started something that has been a bit of a pain for Jane over the years. She would sit and scratch my back for what seemed like ages and I enjoyed it so much that it became something that was hard to live without; now Jane has been tasked with the job on countless occasions, and there have been even greater countless occasions when I have been rebuked upon asking! Now weaned off!

Our home at 64 Coronation Avenue, Keynsham, was certainly different, particularly in size. Mum and Dad had their own bedroom, as did Nan, while John and I shared the third bedroom. Obviously, the bathroom must have been an amazing improvement for the adults. It also meant that having a bath no longer meant bringing in the tin bath to the lounge, together with boiling up water to put in it, a process regularly enacted at 139 City Road! We now had the ubiquitous through lounge and a reasonably sized kitchen, with a nice garden to the rear. I think I followed after my dad regarding our interest in gardening – neither of us had any such interest! Our neighbours were Mr and Mrs Bryant to one side and Mr and Mrs Ranger to the other.

Not too long after we moved, my dad became unwell and was off sick for some time, and clearly times were difficult as we approached Christmas that year. Then one teatime we had a visit from Dad's boss. He came bearing two large chickens and presented them to Mum for Christmas dinner. She was overjoyed. It was a great weight off of her mind. Despite all this, I never remember going hungry. Whether Mum went hungry to ensure we had enough, I shall never know now. I hope not. Sadly, Dad's boss took his own life in the office one day using a handgun. Thankfully, Dad was still off sick, as the bullet continued on through a glass screen into his office!

In Keynsham I was enrolled in the nearest school, Kelston Road Primary School (now gone but replaced by St Keyna Primary), and I settled in quite well. I made friends with a lad called Jeff White, who I sadly lost touch with for some time after secondary school but, thanks to the South African Telephone Directory being online, found many years later. The school was probably post-war and sat on the edge of a marshy field, because at that time much of what is Keynsham today was just undeveloped fields. Indeed, there was little development beyond our house. However, as time went on, Park Estate, as it was called, began to grow. Thankfully, perhaps because of the interview system to get to Keynsham, it was a nice estate and did not have the sort of problems that some other Bristol estates experienced even at that time.

Just around the corner from us they were building St Francis Church in Warwick Road and blocks of council flats, and as kids it was great to go to the building site and build dens from the bricks and use straw as flooring. We would sit inside for ages and amuse ourselves. Roofing was provided by bits of corrugated metal or board – so much for Health and Safety in those days. Funnily enough, also in those days we did not seem to have a need to cause disorder or commit crime, despite having little to do.

I was only at Kelston Road for a year or so before taking and failing the eleven-plus examination, and therefore Keynsham Grammar School did not beckon for me. It was off to Broadlands Secondary Modern, a school with a bit of a negative reputation, but it was not too bad. The major difference in moving from junior to senior is that in one move you go from being the big boy to being the little boy again. It also meant that virtually all kids went from short trousers to long trousers, except for one lad from Whitchurch, who was the exception, continuing in short trousers for a year or two, despite being the tallest lad in the year group.

I very much enjoyed the sports at Broadlands. I took part in the athletics, and while I was no distance runner, I did well in the sprints and even better over the 100-yard hurdles. We played football and I represented the school on a number of occasions.

Sports Day.
From the left: me, unknown but Philip Stapleton rings a bell. Chris Wiltshire, Keith Wood, Ken Maddox, unknown, unknown, and in the background is a wonderful man called Mr Tuddenham, the maths and sports teacher.

We had a headmaster called Mr Richard Morley, a very nice and very fair man who I had great respect for. I know he had had some input into the presence of the thirteen-plus examination at the school. This examination gave dullards like me a second chance to move away from the secondary modern school to something seen to be better. So it was that I sat this examination, and much to my surprise I was successful. Also successful at the same time were Chris Wiltshire, who went on to be an oncology consultant, Robert Ashley, who became a scientist but sadly died too young, perhaps in his late forties/early fifties, my mate Jeff White, who became a geologist and went to live in South Africa, and Dennis Payter, who latterly became an editor with the *Bristol Evening Post*. Somewhere along the line I seem to have messed up. Or did I?

The result of our success saw all of us, apart from Dennis, going off to Bath Technical School; Dennis went to an agricultural college near Bridgwater.

In the summer holidays before the move to Bath Technical School I became ill and had to be hospitalised in Ham Green Hospital. I remember our GP, Dr Munro, telling my mum, withing my earshot, that he thought it might be polio. Suddenly, my imagination went into overdrive, with frightening images of iron lungs for the rest of my life. Once at Ham Green Hospital, they thought it was meningitis, but thankfully after a month it was decided it was viral flu. When I think back to how far Ham Green is from Keynsham and how difficult a bus journey it was, or indeed even a car journey in the doubtfully reliable cars that Dad could afford, I see that Mum and Dad made unbelievable efforts to visit me very often and at times daily, or perhaps it *was* daily. I remember doing lots of painting and crayoning and I was also introduced to basket making by the occupational therapist, as I spent virtually the whole month in splendid isolation.

During my early teens we used to play football in the garage complexes around the council estate, using the garage doors as goal mouths. The downside was that the doors were metal roller shutter doors, and when you scored, the noise was obviously horrendous, as nearby residents made clear when chasing us away. So, a resolution was needed. Some parents suggested a petition to the council, so I gathered a group of friends together and organised a petition, which we collected door to door. This achieved both newspaper and television news coverage. Once completed I went with my dad to the Keynsham Urban District Council offices, where we had a meeting with the town clerk, George Ashton. The outcome was very positive and the council provided a playing field and a pair of goal posts, and that facility remains today some sixty years on, at Kelston Road. My first bit of public service/politics.

Briefing the petition-collecting team. Christine Ranger is on the right.
In the front row is my brother, John, biting his nails. On his left is Martin Hunt, with
Colin Rossiter to his left. Behind John is John Hillier. The two tall lads at the back are
Norman Williams, on the left (now living in Australia), and Robert Cave. On Norman's
right is Jeff White and in the hooped sweater is Daryl Bowden.

Fully recovered, I moved to Bath Technical School and took up the education that should have sealed my success in life. We were in the newly repurposed school building at Brougham Hayes, the first intake on the site. The school is now Hayesfield Girls' School. The entrance examination had been taken at Weymouth House, the old school, in the middle of the city of Bath.

Again, sport played a big part in my life. In athletics I again took to the track over the 100- yard hurdles and set a new school record. On the rugby field I played lock forward and had a trial for Bath Boys, the first step towards England Boys, but unfortunately fractured my wrist in the trial and thus never got anywhere near Twickenham! I played wicketkeeper for the school cricket team. The academic work was not quite as successful. I did not enjoy studying, nor homework, and I eventually reaped the result of that.

Jane and the More Recent Family

I was on my way home from school by bus and was standing in Temple Street at the bus stop waiting for the bus to the estate. Just across Temple Street is the junction with Rock Road, and there in the mouth of Rock Road, waiting to enter Temple Street, was a lovely young girl in her grammar school uniform on a pedal cycle. As she moved off and came past us, the one thing that stood out were her legs. Not for the reason you might think but because they had ink marks on them. Hence, ever since, Jane has been the 'girl with the inky legs'. Love at first sight.

Christine Jane Neal was born on Christmas Eve in 1948 in Cardiff to Victor Henry John Neal, a police officer, and Ilma Price Neal, also a police officer. While she was still very young, the family – she had a younger brother, Christopher John Neal – moved to Uganda, where Victor became an inspector in the Uganda State Police. After some time they returned to the UK and lived initially in South Marston, just outside Swindon – where Victor worked for a local company – until moving into Courtlands, Keynsham, with the family. It was while there that Jane appeared on her bike and I was smitten.

The first time I actually met her was when we were both out with friends at the Charlton Cinema and I fortunately ended up sitting next to her. It was an interesting courtship because we never saw the end of a film at the cinema, as Jane had to be home by 10 pm. One Saturday evening, we went to a dance at Saltford Hall, and while there, there was a fight. The police attended and were still outside when Jane and I left early enough to walk to the bus stop to be in by 10 pm. Unfortunately, the bus failed to turn up and the next one came some one hour later. There were no mobile phones then, so we were not able to let anyone know, and because of the late time, Jane's dad had set out to look for us going to the hall and witnessing the police presence outside. We eventually caught the bus to High Street and I walked Jane home. The following day her dad presented himself at my home, 64 Coronation Avenue, telling my parents that I should never again darken his doorstep. After not too long I mustered the courage to go down to Courtlands and offer my apologies.

After a couple of years the Neal family moved to Tyntesfield Estate, where Jane's dad became chauffeur to Lord Wraxall and the family had a tied cottage adjacent to the stables, so my motorcycle came in handy to visit after work and at weekends. Tyntesfield House and Estate is now owned by the National Trust.

Victor then secured the job of maintenance manager at the world-renowned Liberty of London in Regent Street. So, on the first weekend after they had moved to London he collected me and drove to London, to Jane's grandparents in Hackney, where the family were initially staying. At the end of the weekend he drove me to Victoria Coach Station and bid me a firm goodbye, perhaps hoping that would be the last he would see of me. However, for Jane and I, our long-distance love continued as we managed to write letters on a daily basis and phone each other, from the red public call box of course. I cannot help but wonder how much easier it might have been with email, FaceTime and Skype.

So at least once a month I would be on my 90cc Honda travelling to East Finchley to the maisonette the family now rented at the top of Archway Road – 120 miles away. This task, I used to undertake on my little Honda 90, a similar model to the photo, though I had the luxury of a pannier rack. My hands on a cold day would be dead by the time I had reached Box, to the east of Bath, with still 100 miles to go. Suitcase on the pannier rack and no puncture-repair kit or tool kit, and thankfully never needed either. I do not know whether it was love or stupidity, but Jane is still with me. But then again, I cannot work the washing machine!

Jane, her jobs and our homes

When Jane left school she became PA to the dispatch manager at Liberty. She could type but could not do shorthand. Equal opportunities? Nepotism reigned back then! However, it worked well because when I had a couple of days off I would travel up to London to stay. I would then meet Jane at lunchtime. Just down the road was the BBC Paris Theatre and they would record or broadcast lunchtime or weekend shows that were free to get into, so back then we got to see the likes of Sonny and Cher, the Animals, the Kinks and Lulu, to name but a few. Around the corner from Liberty is Carnaby Street, and then, in the Swinging Sixties, it was the epicentre of flower-power fashion.

Jane and I became engaged on Christmas Eve 1966, on her eighteenth birthday. The other success that year pales into insignificance, but for those not sure what that was, it was the year England played Germany in the World Cup Final, and of course England won – but have never managed to repeat that achievement since.

Sadly, around that time Jane's mum and dad were having a difficult time and heading for separation, and one weekend, after a very heated argument, her mum told Jane that if she wanted to leave with me and come to Keynsham, she could. No need to repeat the offer; Jane packed a case and we went immediately to Victoria Coach Station and travelled back to Keynsham feeling very happy. Sadly, however, within an hour or two at most, Jane's dad was at the front door of my folks' house and her mum was in the car. He had driven straight down and demanded that she return with them, which sadly she felt she had to. Jane's dad was a very strong character.

It was not a long time after that that Jane's parents split up, and at that time Jane came down to stay in my home with my folks. Jane managed to get a job in the offices of Godwin Warren, an engineering company on the Brislington Trading Estate. This was where she was working when we got married on 9 March 1968 – always a popular month to get married, because if you became a married couple within the fiscal year, you received a big refund of tax. Our wedding took place in St John's Parish Church, High Street, Keynsham, and the reception was a roast dinner at the Wingrove public house, Queens Road, in the skittle alley, a very nice community neighbourhood pub at the time (now the Co-op store).

As Jane had recently been living in London and I had regularly visited, the honeymoon was a bit of a busman's holiday: we stayed in the Russell Hotel, London, for a few nights. As I recall, we went to the theatre twice, once to see Gerry Marsdon (Gerry and the Pacemakers – who?) in *Charlie Girl* and then to see *The Black and White Minstrel Show*, very big at the time but later deemed racist. After one of the shows we had a meal, and for the rest of the night I was very unwell in the stomach area! The things you remember. This was compounded by the bathroom not being en-suite but at the end of a corridor.

We returned from London to our first home together, a two-room flat in the loft of 13 Greville Road, Bedminster. One room we lived in and the other we slept in. On the landing we had a sink and a cooker and, as I recall, that was the extent of the kitchenette. We shared the bathroom and toilet one floor below with our landlords.

After not very long we found a flat in Broadlands House, Keynsham, at the top of St Francis Road. Again this was a two-room flat but with a nice big living room and a view out over the Keynsham Hams. The back room was a big bedroom and we had a proper, if small, kitchen. Unfortunately, we still had to share a toilet and bathroom on the half-landing with the three other flats. It was a nice little community though.

Here we needed furniture, and Jane's dad, as the maintenance manager of Liberty in London, the aforementioned world-famous department store, had the job of disposing of furniture that had been used on the shop floor. We became the owners of a drop-leaf oak dining table, six wheelback chairs, including two carvers, a lovely carved-oak ships chest, which we have to this day, and delightful yellow curtains! Hire purchase bought us a three-piece suite, a bed and a hanging wardrobe set.

However, for some while, indeed since our engagement, we had our names on the Keynsham Urban District Council housing list, and it was not long before we were given a flat in Warwick Road – number 56 as I recall – but I cannot remember whether it was A, B or C. It was on the top floor but quite nice. It was there that we stayed up all night with our black and white television on 20 July 1969 to watch the moon landing. As I write this I realise that we were probably only in Greville Road for a month (despite having paid rent for several months in advance to secure the flat) and probably less than a year at Broadlands House.

It was also around this time that Jane became pregnant with Sarah and was most worried that she was going to fall down the concrete stairs in the Warwick Road flats. Amazingly, we were transferred to a two-bedroom house at 21 Lulworth Road, Keynsham, where she promptly fell down the stairs. We were there by the time Sarah was born. This was a terrible house, so bitterly cold, and we ended up burning a one-bar electric fire in the smaller bedroom to keep Sarah warm, as she would not keep her hands under the cover. We had no central heating but had a paraffin heater, which as I recall was quite efficient. How life has progressed!

Clare was born almost three years later, and by that time we had moved again, this time into a brand-new three-bedroom house in

St John's Court, Keynsham. Young people now have no chance of having such a swift transition through the housing ladder for a social house (as they are now called – not council houses). I often wonder whether our swift passage through the system was in any way helped by the housing officer Mr Webb, who was a retired policeman. Surely not!

St John's Court was a lovely new development, and for the first time we had central heating: oil-fired, hot-air central heating. That was fine for the first six months to a year, until there was an oil crisis in the Middle East and the price of oil went through the roof and we could not afford to burn it. We had to go to the nearby builders' merchants, where we bought a Superser gas heater, with fire bricks at the front where the flames were and a bottle of Calor Gas in the back. We pushed it from room to room as needed and lugged it upstairs for the evenings and nights. Happy days!

The Convulsions

It was while we were at St John's Court that Clare had the first of a series of convulsions. Quite frightening initially. She had one during the night and Jane volunteered to go to the telephone box a quarter of a mile away, such was her fear, to summon the doctor. The doctor declined to come!

Sometime after that we managed to buy tickets for Steel Eye Span (who!) at the Colston Hall, Bristol, and my mum was babysitting. During the interval after the support act I rang my mum, only to find that Clare had had another convulsion, so we went home and never did see the main attraction.

One teatime when Jane was working and I had the girls, Clare suffered yet another convulsion, which persisted. I gathered up the girls, ran next door to the Sayers, our lovely neighbours, pushed Sarah through the door to Barbara and told Harry to jump into the car. I then put Clare in his arms, which I think frightened him a bit, and we set off for the Bristol Children's Hospital, with the car headlights of my old two-tone blue automatic Mk1 Cortina full on and my hand pressing the horn. I had hoped to find a police patrol car at Hicks Gate, where they often sat, so they could escort us, but no such luck. We got there safely, and once we had handed Clare into the care of the clinicians, we realised that Harry had come without shoes! He was all for making his own way home on the bus, even without shoes. Jane had been summoned from work and eventually we got Harry home. The clinicians did their work, because, as I recall, that was the last convulsion Clare suffered.

The one positive outcome from Clare's condition was that we were prioritised to have a telephone installed (hence how I was able to ring my mum), albeit a party line shared with a neighbour. I suspect such things as party lines no longer exist, and most people now have a personal mobile anyway.

The collision

In around 1972/73 I was on motorcycle patrol in the Bower Ashton area of Bristol when a young guy in a minivan decided not to stop at a stop sign and came straight out in front of me. I collided with the side of the vehicle. I remember sliding along the road, the road surface passing rapidly, not far from my face, as my crash helmet took the brunt of the impact. Initially, I went by ambulance to the Bristol Royal Infirmary A &E Department, but I came out as walking wounded. However, this collision seems to have been the trigger for the start of my ankylosing spondylitis (AS). After it was diagnosed I started a claim against the errant young driver. After many different medical examinations and a lot of correspondence, the outcome was damages of £2,500, which was a tidy sum at that time. We got our priorities right and bought … a music centre! Then we decided we ought to take to the property market, and so it was that we got a mortgage and bought 4 Corfe Crescent, Keynsham. We were only there for about eighteen months when, due to neighbour issues, we moved to 6 Glebe Walk, in the town.

This was a lovely house, very conventional and lovely neighbours. It was an end terrace and our living and dining rooms were on the outer side of the house. Down that outer side was an amenity green. There were lots of children and the green was the playing field, so footballs were frequently kicked against the outer wall of the house and the impact could be heard inside. Our garden wall at the front was but a metre from our front window and children would sit on the wall despite being asked not to. Eventually, after a few years, we had had enough and started looking around for another house.

We eventually found one just around the corner at 91 Lays Drive. Initially, we believed we could not afford Lays Drive, but the estate agent told us to go and look, and the price was lower than expected. Mr Griffey, the vendor, had been let down by someone who had offered to buy and had lost the flat he'd wanted in Weston-super-Mare. We offered him his asking price and he accepted. The house sold itself when I stepped out into the back garden to encounter a view that blows my mind to this very day. I went out into the back garden and there, laid out in front of me to the east, was a 9-mile view to Bath University and a skyline that starts at Burnet and travels through to beyond Tog Hill, South Gloucestershire, and a goodly proportion of that view was later designated as part of the Cotswolds. What a God-given gift, and that came free with the house! When we were going through the purchase process, our vendor told us that a near neighbour had offered him the same price to move a relative in, and when he had declined, they attempted to 'gazump' us, offering over the asking price, but he was a gentleman and had told them he had agreed a deal and would not change. So on 13 July 1983 we moved in and have lived there ever since.

So that covers our homes, but how about Jane? Well, she has been a great mum, latterly a great nan, a great homemaker and a lovely wife. Having started work for Godwin and Warren, an engineering company, she then managed to secure a post with Martins Bank in the High Street, Keynsham, and later a bookkeeping role with Peter the Baker in Charlton Road. However, it seems that Jane was destined for greater things, and while initially starting a job as an auxiliary nurse at Keynsham Hospital, her mind was set on becoming a nurse. However, she needed to have GCSEs, and so over two or three years at night school she studied and achieved an A* in English and that was followed by passes in psychology and human biology. I was very proud of my wife.

With the necessary qualifications, Jane began her training as a State Enrolled Nurse at the Royal United Hospital, Bath. During her two years of training, the one place she feared being sent to on placement was the A & E Department. However, fate took a hand and it was to A & E that Jane was sent. Much to her amazement, she took to it like the proverbial duck to water. Towards the end of her placement there was a vacancy on the department and she applied. Then one day Jane was sitting in the canteen when one of the regular A & E nurses came to her and said jokingly, 'It's all your fault that I have to stay on until after Christmas.' When Jane asked why, she was told by the nurse that A & E were waiting for Jane's qualification to be ratified and were holding the post open until she was fully qualified. Again I was very proud of Jane's achievement, and for the next nineteen years she had a great life there. It was broken slightly when she had to do a two-year course to qualify as a State Registered Nurse, as the Enrolled role was being phased out. Also, when she went back, they had changed the system. Previously, they had had night workers and day workers; they had now put everyone on a rolling shift system. Nights used to cripple Jane; she would get into bed by 8 am and was lucky if she slept until midday. She was dead on her feet by the Thursday. Then after a week of nights they had five days off and Jane would take until the following Thursday to get back into the land of the living.

However, she loved the work and had a great leader in Senior Charge Nurse Pete Fox, a lovely man.

All went well until Jane's dad was given just two weeks to live. We learnt this on the Monday and Jane and her brother went that evening to see him in London. When she returned she was looking towards two night shifts. As a result, she went to see the charge nurse (not Pete Fox) who was at that time involved in arranging the shifts and explained the impending death of her father and asked if she could move to a day shift in case she had to leave quickly. His response was a 'no' and that 'he had twelve positions to fill already that week' – definitely not the compassionate answer, but that was his problem, not Jane's. As a result, and because of her dedication, she stayed on the two nights, but on the first night she had two male patients die and was obviously distraught. Being more compassionate, the acting sister that night told her to go home and stay home the following day. Jane then went to the doctor, who signed her off with anxiety due to her father's impending death.

Prior to this situation, Jane had been asked whether she would be interested in a job-share on a promotion. She had of course said yes. Well, the 'caring profession' decided to advertise the job, shortlist the applicants, conduct interviews and appoint while Jane was off sick. During that time not one member of management and not one of her colleagues made contact with her to tell her about the job being advertised.

This was the last straw for Jane and she reluctantly resigned, as this had been her dream job, one that would have given her great job satisfaction. Instead Jane went to work on the nursing bank for health centre treatment rooms in and around Bristol. Even then, though, when she gave the name of two senior sisters as references, one of them failed to furnish such a reference, even when requested a second time. Sister Mandy Rumble furnished a glowing reference for Jane in a very short space of time. A while later, when I challenged the other senior sister as to why she had chosen not to provide a reference, she denied having received it – twice! Some are born to lead, and others not!

So Jane became one of the nurses working in the treatment room at Whitchurch Health Centre on the edge of Bristol. When she came home on the first day, she said, 'Guess what I had today?' The answer: a coffee break and meal break – such things were often a bit of a luxury in A & E.

While at the health centre, Jane started working casually for a firm of solicitors as a health records analyst. This was something she enjoyed and continued into retirement. Though sometimes exasperated by her computer, she was very good at what she did and I saw emails and memos from solicitors and barristers commending her on her work. Yet again I was so very proud of what she did and how professional and skilled she was.

It was, as you recall, towards the end of my school life that I first saw Jane on her bicycle at the end of Rock Road, with her inky legs, but it was without doubt love at first sight. I was and have been a very lucky man – more so than I deserve.

Back to the Life Story

As I was approaching the time when I would be leaving school, the only possible career I had in mind was a fireman. My dad had been a fireman during the Second World War, as he was too old for the armed services. When I mentioned the fire service at a career's afternoon at Bath Technical School, the gentleman presenting looked down his nose at me and suggested I should raise my aspirations – a rather sad approach when trying to help young people into employment.

One day I was in the High Street in Keynsham when I bumped into my old headmaster, Mr Richard Morley. We began to talk and he asked what I intended to do. I told him I did not really have anything in mind. He looked me up and down and then said, 'You're a big lad. Why don't you try the police force in the cadets?'

I thought to myself, *Why not? I suppose I could try it.* I hopped on a bus and went into Bristol and collected some pamphlets and an application form from the police headquarters in Bridewell Street. I filled out the application and obtained the three required references: one from Mr Morley, as he seemed a natural choice (it had been his idea); one from the local chimney sweep, Joe Harding; and the third from my then acting headmaster, Mr Hayman (he gave me a glowing reference, saying how in the coming summer exams I would be taking eight O Level GCEs and stood an excellent chance of complete success). On the strength of the references and my interview with the then chief constable, George Twist, I was accepted into the Police Cadet Corps of the Bristol Constabulary. This was just as well because although I took eight GCEs, I managed to fail the lot!

Life's next step

This was the start of my adult life and the end of my life as a schoolchild. While it was exciting to enter the former, it was sad to leave the latter – the world of few responsibilities, of total care from my parents – but fortunately I was still able to live at home. What did the world hold in store for Alan Hale, Cadet 16?

My Family Whom I Love Very Much

My beloved wife, Jane, 'the girl with the inky legs'.

My lovely and much-loved eldest daughter, Sarah

My other lovely and equally loved daughter, Clare.

Cory, a deputy general manager in a cocktail bar in Lincoln.

Mitchell, established in the world of cyber security.

Leah, a dedicated carer in residential care.

Molly, a team leader in adult special needs.

I began the book with a photo of my beloved grandchildren and it seems appropriate in 2022 in order to make the book complete I add photos of them now. May God give me many more years with all of them.

Harry, an apprentice electrician.

The Police Service

The Cadets

I suppose it could be said that I never experienced anything other than a disciplined environment for most of my working life: from school, a place of rules and expectations, to the police service, with more of the same.

It was perhaps strange to suddenly be part of such a wonderful and proud organisation. I certainly wore my uniform with immense pride, despite the rather shapeless cap I was given. It was also a first for me to wear a collarless shirt, kept in touch with the starched collar by an uncomfortable couple of collar studs. Sergeant Tom Perkins was the tailoring sergeant, a somewhat austere man to me as a 16-year-old lad. Perhaps I should have drummed up the courage to tell him the collar was too tight. At least then I would not have had to suffer a permanent stud mark on my throat!

One benefit of joining was that they taught me to swim, thus making the future holidays more fun! I later achieved the Bronze Medallion in lifesaving! I have to say I did not enjoy the early morning training sessions at Jacobs Wells swimming baths in Hotwells Bristol. If you managed to get yourself excused, you ended up in what I think was the boiler room sorting out the old uniforms used for lifesaving training. My recollection, with the benefit of hindsight, was that there was a fair bit of asbestos about in that room!

How did I get to work? Well, before I started with the cadets, I had been the 'sticker up' at the Wingrove pub's skittle alley and had saved the wage to the extent that I bought a nice bright, red, brand-new Honda 50. I believe it cost about £50 at the time. Shortly after, I passed my motorcycle test and gained a full licence. The nonsense at that time was that having passed on a 50cc automatic clutch machine I was then allowed to ride a much larger engined motorcycle.

There is not too much to relate regarding the cadet years. Most of my time was spent office bound, as I served, firstly, in the criminal records office (CRO) and then in the print room under PC Cyril Bishop, followed by a spell in the photographic department under PC Tony Griffiths and, if I remember correctly, Sergeant Wheeler.

Sport and fitness played the biggest part in the cadet's life and we were all under the care and leadership of a wonderful man called Stan Bushen, the sergeant in charge of cadets and their training. A man who, when I met him in the street some eighteen years later – when I was on motorcycle patrol and encased in a full-face crash helmet and he was well into his old age – immediately upon looking at me said, 'It's young Hale'. If ever there was a man who should have had a Civil List honour, it was Stan Bushen. Stan was the man who provided the police service with some of its finest officers, many of whom went on to be senior officers and at least one a chief constable, Dirk Aldous in Dorset. Okay, so arguably his magic did not work on me!

The worst few weeks of my cadetship came very early on when we had to go on Junior Camp. Three weeks – it might have been two but seemed like three – of torture for me. It was only just outside of Bristol, on the A38, at what is now the Woodhouse Park Activity Centre, but it was winter and under canvas. I found myself having to do lots of things for myself that my mum normally did: washing, washing-up, cooking, etc! A fair bit of hiking was also required.

Assault courses seemed to feature high on the list, particularly the one at the police Kings Weston sports ground, near Lawrence Weston, Bristol, where we had to negotiate two- and three-rope bridges that climbed high into the trees, probably up to 50 feet, then descended on a pulley-and-rope zipwire line. Character-building was probably the name of the game. The interesting part was that throughout all of the rope work, we never had a safety harness, safety net, or anything similar. This was a time before Health and Safety took hold of common sense around the neck and hung on until it was stifled.

Cresswell Heath. Clive Hipken, Ricky Hook, me and Barry Perkins at Junior Camp, Woodhouse.

I represented the cadets at football as goalkeeper and also played for the full Bristol Constabulary team in a league. It was this clash of loyalties that got me into trouble one day. I was supposed to be playing for the cadets in the morning and the force team in the league in the afternoon. Probably because I did not have spare kit, I decided I could not play for both, so did not turn up for the cadet match! On the following Monday Inspector Callaghan, the training inspector at the training school in Clifton, Bristol, pointed out, in a loud and firm way, the error of my ways and something about being a 'bloody prima donna'!

Me at half time in a very muddy football game. Sergeant Stan Bushen has his back to the camera and Barry Powell is on the right of the photo

At about the same time, I played for a Keynsham team in the Bath under-18 league. I was successful enough to be selected as goalkeeper for a representative team from the league and we played Bristol Rovers' under 18s side at Eastville Stadium. We lost, but it was quite an experience playing in an actual league stadium. I also had a couple of games in goal for Keynsham Town, saving a penalty in one of the matches.

Suspected of burglary

One event while attached as a cadet to East Street Police Station CID came close to trouble. It was the practice in the cadets to slash the peak of your cap so it came down over your eyes, and also to set the front of the cap up with something forced behind the front bracing bar. I was no different. One morning, with little to do in the CID office, I decided I would renew the material behind the bracing bar. So I pulled out the folded piece of card and replaced it with something more substantial. Job done!

A day or so passed, then one evening at home there was a knock at the door; I was at home with Dad. I went to the door and to my surprise met two detectives from the CID office I was attached to. They were equally surprised to see me and asked to come in. I let them in and they asked my dad to leave us. They then asked me, 'Do you know anyone in Southville?'

'No,' was my reply.

They then asked me if I knew a particular woman whose name they gave.

'No,' was again my reply.

'Are you sure you don't perhaps have a girlfriend you have had an argument with?'

'No. I have a girlfriend, but not in Southville,' I replied.

'Well, we have found your name and address on a document in the contents of a handbag stolen from her house in a burglary.'

I started to get worried, despite being totally innocent. They continue to ask questions, and as they did so one of the detectives was holding a card in his hands and folding and unfolding it again and again.

Then it suddenly clicked and I recognised the document as the card I had removed from my cap a couple of days earlier. When I explained this, it became apparent that they had brought the bag back to the office and turned out the contents onto the desk – obviously, the desk I had used and had left the card on. How close can you get to a wrongful conviction?

The have-nots

It was in the cadets that I realised one morning that many people lead very deprived lives. We were, as a body, taken off training to help in the search for a missing child in the Southmead Estate. We were paired up with officers to go and search neighbouring houses. Where a missing child is concerned, the search always starts at the child's home and works its way out. I was amazed as we went into house after house where there was nothing on the floors, little in the cupboards, and the bedclothes consisted of overcoats thrown down on bare mattresses – quite an eye-opener. As a family, we did not have a lot, but clean bedding and some floor covering were always evident.

Cadet Day was an annual event attended by parents to witness their child's development at the hands of Sergeant Bushen. It began with a marching display, always to the music of the Royal Air Force March Past. That was a proud moment. We would then get changed into our gym kits and give displays of unarmed combat, assault-course work and gymnastics. One year, Cadet Barry Perkins came off the vaulting horse awkwardly and broke his neck. Fortunately for Barry, he made a full recovery and went on to become a sergeant; fortunately for the police service, we were not yet then in the blame culture, suing for anything and everything. Sadly, Barry died an untimely death from cancer in, I believe, 2008.

Mobile column

In the early 1960s we were still very much part of the Cold War and the so-called Iron Curtain was still in place. The threat of nuclear war was also ever-present. In answer to that threat, the Home

Office put in place, albeit not permanently, the Police Mobile Column. This consisted of a convoy of large trucks. Inside each truck was a central table with wooden benches on either side. Each truck would carry a sergeant and about six or seven constables. The convoy was commanded by a chief superintendent who travelled with a driver in a Land Rover. There were also motorcycle outriders and a cadet – that was me – in one of the trucks. The idea, as I understood it, was that in the event of a nuclear attack, this convoy would be staffed and would somehow or other police on the move. I assumed that there would be such a convoy in each police district.

We would take part in various exercises over a period of a fortnight, driving around many counties in the south-west from the army camp where we were based, in Devizes. The Army Catering Corps took care of our meals, and what a great job they did.

Probably the funniest spectacle, although with hindsight perhaps upsetting to some, was when the decision was made that a 'wee' break was required by the convoy of some seven to ten vehicles. As you might expect, cars often got caught up in the convoy, so as the whole thing started to slow to a halt on a suitable country road, they too would come to a halt as some forty or more police officers suddenly dismounted and lined up on the hedge side of the trucks and did the necessary. I do not think anyone complained, perhaps more by luck than judgement!

During the fortnight, we actually got to respond to a real need. The Verne at Portland Bill was a prison or similar for young offenders, and while out on a working party, two prisoners had attacked a prison officer and escaped. However, there is only one road off the 'Bill' and so it was not a problem to contain them but they had to be found and recaptured. So off we went at as high a rate of knots as was possible, with our outriders stopping traffic at junctions to see us through, bound for the beautiful county of Dorset.

When we arrived at Portland Bill we drove up into the car park at the viewing point that looks back along Chesil Beach and the Jurassic coastline, now designated a World Heritage Site. Well worth a visit. However, when I opened the rear swing doors of our truck, I did not appreciate how foul the weather was, nor the strength of the wind. The door was ripped from my grasp as it swung away and smashed against the side of the truck. To this day I give thanks to the fact that no one was in the way. It would surely have resulted in a fatality.

Many wet and windy hours were spent searching the Portland stone quarries, getting wetter and filthier by the minute. I do not recollect whether one of our convoy found them; indeed, I do not know whether they were found on that day. What I do know for certain is that the temperature was near freezing and the sleet was falling heavily. My recollection is that it was late afternoon when we set off back to Devizes. We were perhaps halfway back when it was decided that the motorcycle outriders were at risk due to the road conditions and were certainly suffering badly from the cold, so our truck was one of those that ended up having a 500cc Triumph motorcycle heaved into the back. Its rider also joined us and I suspect he found it little warmer in the back of the truck than he had outside. I slept for most of the remainder of the trip. Back at camp we were all welcomed with hot tots of rum. I am not much of a drinker of alcohol but that certainly went down well and was extremely warming. We then tucked into a fine meal, courtesy of the Army Catering Corps.

The Duke of Edinburgh Award

With Dad at Buckingham Palace, having received my Duke of Edinburgh Gold Award.

Probably the high point of my cadetship was my achievement of the Duke of Edinburgh Gold Award and a trip to Buckingham Palace to receive it from the duke himself. Sadly, at that time only one parent could accompany each recipient, so Mum stayed at home. With the early and untimely death of my dad a year or two later, I am pleased that he did in fact come with me. Mum had many more years to, hopefully, be proud of me.

The expedition was perhaps the most challenging, with four nights out (or was it three but felt like four?) on Dartmoor. We started near Tavistock and went all over the moor, camping at night, as I recall, in bivouacs. I had taken my transistor radio with me and was carrying it in the chest pocket of a far-from-waterproof anorak. When we were met by the expedition monitors at one point in the pouring rain, I asked whether they could take care of the radio for me, and it took a bit of begging before they agreed. 'Well, you started with it, so you should finish with it.'

Another part of the programme was the project or hobby. In the book of choices was 'Film Appreciation'. Thinking this would be a good choice, I went down to the Charlton Cinema in Charlton Road, Keynsham, and spoke to the manager, Mr Day. I explained that I had to watch films and write a review of them, and Mr Day had to review my reviews and mark them accordingly. The best part was that Mr Day arranged for me to go in for free when I was doing the reviews, but the lovely outcome from Mr Day's kindness was that Jane and I never had to pay to go into the local cinema again!

Senior Camp

One of the most enjoyable months of my service in the cadets was Senior Camp, four weeks on Exmoor just outside Dunster and under canvas. I had clearly matured since Junior Camp and enjoyed every minute of it. The great sadness during that month was that Nan Hall died aged 84. Inspector Callaghan came down to the camp to give me the news. My nan was a wonderful lady who had been such an enormous part of my life, living with us as she did. A saving grace was that the whole camp had been back the previous week for the Constabulary Swimming Gala and, as she was in hospital, I had been allowed to visit her. Nevertheless, a devastating loss, particularly as I was away. I was given leave to return for the funeral but had to make my own way home! I was driven out onto the main A-road near Dunster and dropped. I managed it by way of hitch-hiking, and made it in five lifts, and then a bus ride from Bristol to Keynsham. Not quite sure why Inspector Callaghan could not have given me a lift on the day he came down. Perhaps it was thought of as character-building having to make my own way back!

I completed my cadetship in June 1966 and on the 13th of that month I became PC 72E as I joined the Bristol Constabulary as a constable. The 'E' number was a training number for my time at Chantmarle, the No. 6 Region Training Centre in Dorset, sadly no longer there – the building is, but not the training centre.

The Police Service

Chantmarle was thirteen weeks of very intense training. Chantmarle itself is an old manor-type house with grounds and a moat, with some newer classrooms at the rear. The sleeping accommodation was rather dormitory in style, with five of us sharing a not- terribly-big room. I was the only one on the intake who did not have to have a haircut upon the first inspection.

I was one of a class of nineteen officers, and there were two classes on the intake. In the photograph below, I am on the front

Me (front row, extreme left), Alan Fox (front row, extreme right) and Barry Lock (back row, extreme right) at Chantmarle. My class instructor, Davey Hulme, is sitting next to me.

row, extreme left, and Alan Fox is on the extreme right. Alan was my best man when Jane and I married, and Barry Lock, extreme top right, was an usher at the wedding. My instructor was a sergeant called Davey Hulme from Exeter City Police; that's him sitting next to me. His summary of the people we were going to encounter was, 'They are all a load of idiots. They have to be, because on the motorway in fog they have to have flashing yellow lights to tell them they cannot see where they are going!' This, in fact, sadly summed up a proportion of the general public quite nicely in my service that followed.

There were many definitions to learn, many powers to memorise and much role play. Self-defence was a bit of a nonsense really because you knew what to expect and the 'opponent' also knew what was going to happen. I do not recall such conformity in various pub fights and public disorder.

The triple police shooting

While at training school, there was a trip to Dorchester for a parade led by the Corps of Drums of Her Majesty's Royal Marines and a memorial service to honour three Metropolitan police officers killed in August 1966 by a criminal called Harry Roberts and his accomplices. The London police officers stopped a van carrying Roberts, John Duddy and Jack Witney as they fled from an armed robbery. Roberts shot Detective Constable David Wombwell dead at point-blank range. He then turned the gun on Sergeant Chris Head, shooting him in the back. Duddy then shot dead the police driver, PC Geoffrey Fox.

Duddy and Witney were arrested quickly but Roberts went on the run for three months. This meant that I had finished my training and had some annual leave to be taken by the time the case came to court. It was during that leave, which I spent in London with Jane, where she continued to live and work, that I was able to sit in on the trial. At the Old Bailey, Mr Justice

PC Geoffrey Fox, 41 (left), Detective Constable David Wombwell, 25 (centre) and Detective Sergeant Christopher Head, 30 (right) were murdered on 12 August 1966.

Glynnes sentenced Roberts to a minimum of thirty years. His criminal record included a seven-year term for beating a man so badly that he later died. He tried to escape twenty-two times and was refused parole in 1996. Witney was murdered in a hostel and Duddy died in jail. Some might say that justice was ultimately served.

Dormitory life at Chantmarle. I am on the left, with Eric Tweddle in the middle, who went on to become a superintendent in the Wiltshire Constabulary. Sadly, I do not remember the name of the man on the right but I believe he was with Devon or Cornwall.

This was justice as it should be, but sadly nowadays such people would perhaps serve fifteen years if they were lucky, whereas the police widows continue to serve a life sentence. It has to be said that the unusual death of the three officers was a frightening way to start one's police career.

The B Division Years

When I joined B Division on my return from training, it was then part of the Bristol Constabulary. On day one I was welcomed by Superintendent Fred Williams, who informed me that the division enjoyed 75 per cent of Bristol's criminals living within its boundaries – probably only a small change to that percentage even now. The division was quite varied, with a number of shopping centres, such as East Street, North Street and West Street. It also had one side of the city docks, and at that time a regular sight saw Russian timber ships tied up. There was industry and Ashton Gate Stadium, the home of Bristol City.

It was while on duty at the stadium at a home match that I saw the lad who had started school at Broadlands in short trousers, but now he was a big guy and I had seen his photograph on a circulation a few weeks back as being wanted for being absent without leave from the Royal Navy. My first step was to go to the police office at the stadium to check that this was still the case, and it was. I then went back to the terraces with a slight degree of trepidation, because he was a big lad, but fortunately, when I said hello using his name and told him I was arresting him and why, he offered no resistance and walked quietly out with me.

I was 'shown around' or, as some forces called it, 'puppy walked', by my tutor, Constable Brian 'Noddy' Taylor. Brian was, and is, a super man with a great sense of humour and a ready laugh. He now lives in retirement in Keynsham, so I meet him occasionally. His cars were something to behold; they were never new but he must have spent hours of loving care on them because the engine was extremely clean and the outside spotless.

I was shown how to check the 'fastenings' on nights. Yes, in those days not only did you have time to check the security of each and every commercial property, but more importantly you were required to. There was also time on nights to take details of all vehicles you saw moving, together with the number of occupants. These details were then entered into the 'Night Movement Book' at the end of the shift – sounds more like a book to record your bowel activity. Times have certainly changed, if in no other way than the volume of traffic moving at night.

On days, you were expected, among your other duties, to visit the public toilets on your patch and note any problems, this in addition to noting any defects in street furniture or potholes in the road, all of which then had to be recorded in a book. You also had to check the property of people who had told the station they would be away on holiday. Again, yet another book to make entries into. Try getting the police to do that today!

Sergeant Sam Mead

On all shifts, you would actually be supervised on the streets by the sergeant. He would come and visit you, spend time with you and walk part of your beat with you. If you were under the supervision of Sergeant Sam Mead, he would meet you at one end of the beat and walk at a great rate to the other end, with you in tow. How times have changed. He ruled with a rod of iron but was a great character who I met a couple of times after his retirement. His funeral was very well attended, always a sign of the respect others hold for the deceased.

An abiding memory of Sam Mead happened one morning, when at the top end of East Street, Bedminster, I stopped a couple of lads, one of whom had an offensive weapon, a knife. I consequently arrested him and put him in the panda car. His mate asked where I was taking him and I told him East Street Police Station. His response was to ask for a lift with his mate. I told him that would not happen. I drove off. A while later, having put the prisoner in the cells, I was in the front office when the mate came in shouting and bawling about not being given a lift. Sam Mead was the station sergeant and was sitting at his desk writing. He looked up and said, 'Show this young man out, PC Hale.' I took hold of his arm, led him to the door and put him out into the street. I was still on the public side of the station front counter when he came back in. Again he started to speak in a raised voice, 'I want to make a complaint.'

'What about?' asked Sergeant Mead.

'Him,' he said, pointing at me.

As I looked towards Sergeant Mead, he gently put down his fountain pen and slowly took off his spectacles, placing them gently on the desk. He then came out from behind his desk and lifted the counter flap, now moving more briskly! 'In that case, you might as well make a complaint against me as well,' said Sam. 'Open the front door, PC Hale,' he continued, and with that he grabbed the complainant by the scruff of his neck and the seat of his trousers and gave him the bums rush down the corridor, past me holding the door. As he ejected the youth, Sam kicked his backside for good measure. Surprisingly, he never came back. Happy days! A different world. Arguably a better world.

The police stations

B Division had four stations at that time: East Street (pictured below), Broadbury Road, St Annes and Knowle. Each station had a character of its own. These were the days when police stations were like hospitals used to be: clean and polished!

East Street was the headquarters station for the division and resembled a castle or fort. All that was missing was the drawbridge, and one of those would have been handy at times.

East Street Police Station

The front office, or station office, was the public face of the service. The station office had a nice impressive wooden counter with a desk behind. This was the domain of the station sergeant and his reserve, the latter being the jailer, the tea maker, the stoker for the central-heating coal-fired boiler, and many other tasks, none of which seemed to extend to actually dealing with anything at the public-facing desk. This was the task of the man on East Street beat who would be summoned by way of the flashing pillar light at the London Inn or the light protruding over the portcullis at the front of the station.

In one corner of the office was the telephone exchange, normally staffed by a female telephonist. It was the typical cables-and-jacks type of exchange. I manned it for a couple of shifts and that was enough!

In the other corner of the office a door led into the charge office, the arrival point for those who had been arrested. It was here that prisoners were booked in and their property removed from them before they were taken away to a cell in the cell block. The East Street cells were like police cells ought to be: dark, cold and uncomfortable. Of course, nowadays you cannot put the poor dears to any discomfort; they must have heating and anything else they need. This despite the fact that anyone in a cell is normally a common criminal who has caused distress to other law-abiding citizens. Yet to be found guilty, of course! At the back end of the twentieth century and the beginning of the twenty-first century the criminals enjoyed the support of various groups – Liberty, for one – because, of course, common criminals have rights: the right to kill, injure, rape, steal, and any other misdeed they choose to commit. What a shame that the victim seems to enjoy little or no rights, and no army of activists to support their rights. How fashionable it must be to represent the interests of the varied ranks of low life that contribute absolutely nothing to society but expect everything back from that same society. Indeed, in the years of austerity in the period around 2014–2020 there were very few police in evidence on the streets. As time moved beyond 2016 the police were selling off the police stations.

In the rear yard, near the rear gate, were the stables, because at that time each division had a mounted detachment: two horses at East Street, with others at St George, Fishponds and Central and the majority at Redland.

Next to the stables was the parade room where we paraded for duty at the commencement of each shift. That parade was always fifteen minutes unpaid before the start of your shift. The parade room was also a cloakroom but left plenty of room for the many officers who then paraded in two or three ranks before the briefing lectern.

'Present your appointments' was the phrase always heard at the start of the briefing. On this command, the supervisor would see every officer standing to attention and holding his truncheon, pocketbook and whistle; on nights, this little list would include your torch. Briefings were always very formal occasions, where you remained in your ranks to listen. There was certainly no likelihood of being invited to sit down, and perish the thought of a cup of tea being enjoyed while you listened. Very much a disciplined organisation. A different world. Arguably a better world!

Further down the rear yard was the policewomen's office. Many years were to pass before WPCs gained equality, and so they remained part of the W Division, dealing with such matters as domestic violence, sexual offences and lost children.

Within the body of the station, at the rear, was the Transport Section. I say 'Transport Section': it was where they kept the pedal cycles. The cycle mechanic 'lived' there. He had the task of ensuring that all of those trusty, heavy, black, upright, ungeared metal pedal cycles were roadworthy. Rank hath its privileges though, as the sergeant enjoyed the luxury of a Sturmey-Archer three-speed gear, while the inspector actually had a car to use. Not having gears did not matter too much, as we rode to the police system of pedal cycling. Very simple really: when the front wheel became higher than the back, you got off and pushed because you were now going uphill!

The CID had a modern detached building in the yard near to the outside toilet.

Upstairs in the station was the divisional police club. Yes, in those days 'the job' encouraged you to socialise with other police officers at the station. There's nothing like a bit of social segregation! That's something that has perhaps not changed, for those who choose it, more's the pity.

I was in the snooker room of the club, playing a game during my breakfast break on early turn, when I got the message that Jane had gone into labour with our first daughter, Sarah. I very quickly leapt into the panda car and drove at great speed to Broadbury Road Station to pick up my own car before rushing to Keynsham Hospital Maternity Unit. I need not have rushed; my mum was already there! Still, I was in plenty of time to be present for the birth and to share the agony of childbirth as my wedding ring was

Our new arrival, Sarah, with a very young Jane and a very slightly older me. I had lost a lot of weight for no known reason. I wish I could manage it now! This photo was courtesy of the police photographer Tim O'Connor, a perfect gentleman who sadly later lost his sight.

Unfortunately, we were unable to achieve such a photo when Clare came along. Pennies were tight and professional photograhers wanted lots of pennies!

squeezed into the skin of my fingers as Jane held my hand! What we men have to go through!

Also on the first floor of the station was the superintendent's office, plus one or two other offices, and then that of the superintendent's clerk. This august position was manned by two PCs, at that time Graham Lock and Dave Bond. They seemed to manage anything and everything that divisional admin, admin support units, prosecutions and a whole host are now employed to undertake. Perhaps the police have lost their way; perhaps they should have stuck to the business of law enforcement and left all other ancillary things to be picked up by someone other than the themselves.

There was also a canteen where you could purchase a cooked meal, certainly breakfast or lunch (no chance now with no police stations). There was a gaming machine too that seemed to be provided specifically for the cook; she certainly put the most money in it and got quite irate if you stepped in while she went away in search of some small change.

Both Knowle and St Annes were as close to a detached beat as you will ever get in the city. The former, at Calcott Road, Knowle, had a station office PC and two patrols. There were only two beats. You turned left at the end of the road, where it met Wells Road, to cover Totterdown and right to cover Knowle and Upper Knowle. It was on the lower beat that I first went solo. Like St Annes, my recollection is mainly of a more relaxed regime and lots and lots of polish. They really did shine. Sadly, I did very little duty at St Annes but I do remember that every late turn, at about 5 pm, the local ice-cream makers would deliver a large block of ice-cream for the men. Perhaps it could be construed as bribery, but you do not like to offend people, so the ice cream was eaten!

On the other hand, Broadbury Road was the 'modern' station on the division. However, it held little attraction for me, I suppose because it did not look like a typical imposing police station. From there you had the task of patrolling Knowle West, or the 'Wild West', as it was called at times.

I think that Knowle was my favourite because, at that time, Totterdown was actually a community twice the size of what it is now, with a thriving shopping centre at The Bush (the pub name sited there), and thus provided scope for good policing. The station PC was Ivor Aish on my shift, and cribbage was what we played at refreshment time. The rest room, as I recall, was directly behind the front desk via a door. As there were two foot patrols, you came in for your refreshments individually, so Ivor had the task of joining us both so that cribbage could be played. Station officer was obviously a challenge! Ivor, though, did a great job.

I was shown around every beat at every station more than once – as was every other probationer – before it was considered appropriate to be released upon the public. That release came on one early tour on the 'lower half' at Knowle. My first self-generated job was to report a driver for failing to give precedence on a pedestrian crossing at The Bush on Wells Road, in the then shopping centre area. The sergeant's first question on giving me a visit was how bad the accident had been. When I explained there had been no accident, he asked me why I had bothered! Some you win ...!

Not to be discouraged, I continued to work hard and patrol diligently, as indeed I was one Sunday morning when working from Broadbury Road. It was Sunday lunchtime as I cycled up Whitchurch Lane near the old airfield. I was overtaken by a car that immediately stopped. It was another PC, an ex-cadet like me.

'Get in the back and have a sit down,' said Ray Shipway (later my superintendent at Bath in the 1990s), out with Mary for the morning. Mary was his girlfriend and later his wife, as well as someone who had been a cadet. Welcoming the opportunity of a rest, I placed my pedal cycle next to the kerb and walked to the rear of the car and got in. Only seconds had passed since I had entered when suddenly the car was violently catapulted into the adjoining airfield via the hedge. Upon emerging somewhat shaken, we found a written-off car in Whitchurch Lane, roughly where Ray's car had been. I later admitted to the inspector, Ralph Rossiter, that I had been engaged in 'idle conversation', a disciplinary offence then. Truthful admission is always good, because that was as far as it went – that is except for the offending driver, who was later convicted of driving without due care and attention and, as I recall, had been drink driving.

I suppose that situation set the benchmark for the rest of my service. A Midas I definitely was not. In fact, many of the things I touched turned to a slightly duller colour, and were certainly less solid than gold.

I moved to Bishopsworth Police Station (photograph below) sometime later. It was a brand-new station, built to replace East Street Station After all, why have a police station in the middle of a very busy commercial and shopping area when you can have one situated almost on the city boundary on a steep hill, just below a

Bishopsworth Police Station

blind brow and just short of a busy crossroads. I suppose the land was cheap and nobody else wanted to build anything in such a vulnerable location. Now, in 2022, there are no police stations, just three custody units, though they do have a front desk, I believe.

Unit Beat Policing

Soon came the Panda Scheme, or to give it its proper title, the Unit Beat Policing Scheme. Each division was divided into units and each unit was patrolled by a panda car, so called because it was painted in broad bands of blue and white; however, I have yet to see a blue and white panda. The new scheme meant that B Division was patrolled by ten cars. Each of the ten units was allocated a detective constable and two or three latter-day community beat officers or, as they are called now, beat managers. Then there were GPPCs (general purpose PCs) to cover the office and to perform foot patrol. The scheme was introduced because of a lack of police officers. What price trying to staff it now. Possibly might manage it with the so-called police community support officers (PCSOs). Probably not.

Like all good police reorganisation, you buy the equipment first and then find that you have got insufficient properly qualified people to make it work. In other words, qualified drivers. This was at a time when police officers, like many others, were travelling to work on buses, motorcycles and pedal cycles.

The driving school

Thus was born the forerunner of the force driving school. Sergeants Doug Reed and 'Iron' Len Oatley together with PCs Abe Bicknell and Sid Wills, were the training staff, plus four black Morris 1000s. In 1968 I passed through the hands of Abe Bicknell, a lovely man, and after three weeks became the proud possessor of a car driver's licence. Another two weeks of training followed and this qualified me to drive a panda.

Pat Bell, me, Gordon Spiers, instructor Abe Bicknell, instructors Len Oatley and Doug Reed and, far right, Sid Wills.

Before I got near a panda, I impetuously went out and bought a Ford Popular with a three-speed gearbox and windscreen wipers that ran off engine compression, so when you really needed them they were very slow and, vice versa, when you did not need them to be fast running they were back and forth across the screen dementedly – not a good purchase. No windscreen washers then, so you kept an old washing-up liquid bottle filled with water near to hand in the car and just wound the window down and reached out and squirted a jet of water onto the screen. However, the really good accessory I installed was a set of Maserati air horns. Now, they really made a noise!

A police driver

Now back to the panda car. What could be better than a blue and white two-door Morris 1000 with a 'Police' sign on top that measured almost 24 inches high, 18 inches deep and was almost the full width of the car. They were not the fastest things on the road, even without the sign. Never mind, I was now a police driver.

With a shoulder number of PC 90B I soon became known as 'Joe 90'. Well, in those days there was no way you could drive properly without sunglasses and black leather gloves! You had to have something to overcome the wind resistance of the roof sign.

You may well wonder how such a vehicle, so equipped, would fare in a chase situation. I only had two. In the first I kept up admirably, but on that occasion it was a Morris 1000 van I was chasing, and the driver had neither sunglasses nor black gloves, so he had no chance. Having covered a couple of miles unaided, I entered the city centre, where I was joined by a Wolseley 6/110 Traffic car driven by the late John Butler. As we continued the pursuit out onto Redcliffe Way, the van tried to sideswipe the big patrol car – big mistake – and in consequence had no trouble spinning out of control.

The second chase was with Charlie Bland as my observer. Without a doubt, Charlie was the nicest, most laid-back policeman I have ever had the pleasure to know. Charlie and I decided to stop a BSA 650 motorcycle 'two up' in Winterstoke Road. I pulled alongside and Charlie waved them to stop. We pulled in in front of it and it rode around us. Now, this happened two or three times and I decided I was doing something wrong. Perhaps I was slowing down too slowly, so the next time we got in front I slowed down much more quickly – much more quickly, in fact, than the motorcyclist, who in trying yet again to go around us struck the rear bumper. Once we had lifted him from the road, he was arrested. Then we put him in the ambulance we had called and conveyed him to the Bristol Royal Infirmary casualty unit. Rather stupidly, he tried to escape and a fight ensued. The result was that he left casualty in a worse state than he had entered. The good old days. A different world. Arguably, a better world!

The panda car came in useful for crowd control on occasions – well, certainly on one occasion. After a Bristol City football match, the usual unruly crowd turned out and a large crowd of disorderly youths went into Ashton Park, and clearly trouble was brewing. So without thinking too much, I drove the car into the park and onto the grass and started to drive through the crowd, changing direction, changing speed, blowing the horn and stopping them from massing in any way. Eventually, they got the message and dispersed.

The following week, I was doing duty at the match when Inspector Bob Cutler came up to me and asked whether I had been the driver of the car in the park. When I said I had been, he passed on the thanks of the superintendent, who thought I had done a great job. A different world. Arguably, a better world!

Communication

Before the police pillar, came the police whistle, and when I joined it was still part of the police uniform. The theory as I understood it was that if you needed assistance from the man on the neighbouring beat, you blew the whistle. Well,

The police pillar, which was to be found on many street corners throughout the city and stood just about 2 metres high, with an orange light on the top that was activated to flash if there was a job for you. Below the light were a couple of doors on a triangular section. One door was for the public to open and contact the police using the telephone therein, and the other door had a lock on it for the policeman, and he too could have a conversation with the station. Inside there was a little fold-out contraption to rest your pocketbook on while you wrote down details of the job.

how hard would you have to blow it to be heard by a man a mile away or more? And if he heard it, which way should he run to help? It begs the question whether it is wise to put a whistle in your mouth if someone is about to punch you there; you would be blowing it for the rest of the night. Perhaps that is why they had it on the end of a chain, so that you might rescue the whistle from the back of your throat!

Within my first two years they introduced two-way radios, and like so many things technical or electrical, when first available they are very big; these were almost the size of a couple of bricks and were worn in a harness on your chest, which was fine if you did not want to breathe deeply. By the end of a shift you felt as though you were being pulled forward. They were then attached to a carrier on your belt, but while this helped you breathe, it did little to make them any lighter.

The Phillips two-way, two-piece radio came next: one part to listen to and the other to speak into. This was a challenge for a policeman! Timing was everything, because the piece you spoke into contained the retracted aerial and to erect it you pressed the transmit button, so it was vital you did that before you got the handset to your face, otherwise there was every chance the aerial would shoot up your nose!

As time went on, the hand-held radios improved and became more user-friendly and reasonably effective.

Yearning for the Traffic Department

As I became more at ease with the motor car, I yearned to become a Traffic man. The first problem was that I had never had a Devizes-standard driving course, Devizes being the No. 6 Regional Police Driving School, hallowed ground as far as driver training was concerned. However, through I assume a lot of hard talking, the No. 6 Regional District Police Driving School decided to accept the Bristol local course as a standard course substitute. Quite frightening really, considering the Bristol school ran a fleet of Morris 1000s, while Devizes ran state-of-the-art, high-powered Wolseley, Austin, Ford and Vauxhall saloon cars. Back then foreign cars were just that: foreign.

I was granted a three-month Traffic attachment. When I first sat behind the wheel of a Wolseley 6/110, I felt completely out of my depth. Here was I, who had never driven anything bigger than a Morris 1000 or Ford Popular, driving a car, the bonnet of which seemed to be as long as a Ford Popular.

On top of that, it was an automatic, as was the entire fleet, bar QR 4, which had a gearstick. Despite three months of such vehicles and my PC mentor instructing me, it was of little help, as all my driving was conducted within the confines of Bristol, where there is a 30-mph speed limit. I occasionally had an opportunity to drive QR 4 but not enough to be of help when the hallowed garages of Devizes became a reality.

The advanced course was a terrible time for me and at the end I failed through lack of experience – which was not surprising – and a not-too-wonderful instructor. However, I was told by the examiner that they would willingly retest me in the future – so bad news, good news. Even before leaving Devizes, I was on the telephone badgering the Traffic Department to give me another chance to gain that all-important 'experience'.

A while later they agreed, and this time I was crewed with, sadly, the now-late, smooth, handsome, suave, silver-tongued George Johnson. What a build-up; a lovely gentleman. This time things were much better. George actually took the trouble to teach me, and to that end we actually went outside the city. In fact, I'm sure I remember drinking tea somewhere in South Wales (Abergavenny, I think). The retest came and I passed. I was now an advanced police driver.

Perhaps my initial failure makes me unique, because from that failure, I went on to qualify as a grade 1 advanced driving instructor many years later.

Having qualified to advanced level, it was Bristol Constabulary's practice to return you to your territorial division to drive Morris 1000s and await selection for G Division, as Traffic was then called. It was a painful wait, during which time I became the community policeman for Southville and the Chessels in Bedminster. That was an interesting time. My community beat was predominantly residential and shops. Of course, at that time almost every police officer was a community officer because that is where they worked – among the community – but the Panda Scheme was working hard at destroying that comfortable position. The policeman was now car-bound for a lot of the time.

The theory of the scheme was that the driver would drive to a location and then alight and carry out foot patrol in the area. While this was a laudable ethos, it did not quite work. As the police were getting to jobs more quickly, now that they were mobile, people were more likely to ring the police, and so more time was spent in the vehicle going from call to call.

This was compounded when there was an oil crisis and, therefore, a mileage restriction on each panda – not very practical when you are trying to do the job. Apparently, some officers used to disconnect the speedometer to keep within the recorded mileage limit for the logbook! Imagine doing that! A different world. Arguably, a better world!

During this interim time, I was constantly going down to Traffic HQ, making a nuisance of myself and urging them to call for my transfer, until I was eventually told by the Traffic superintendent that there were no vacancies and it would be at least eighteen months before I was considered, and even then I might not be successful.

Then fate took a hand. One morning, in the rush hour, I was driving along Bedminster Down when a young lady caught my eye on the far side of the road. I would not normally do this, you understand, but I looked in her direction until she left my line of sight. I looked forward again, only to find the traffic had stopped. I managed to stop okay; however, only after crashing into the back of a Ford Cortina. It was driven by a very nice man who told me that as he only had a cracked light lens, if I wanted to pay for it, he would forget about it rather than get me into trouble. It seemed like a very good idea. That was until I looked at the front of the Morris 1000, the icon of British engineering. There I saw that the bumper was bent and the radiator grill was dented. The radiator was punctured and leaking coolant all over the road! It had to be reported. I had had a blameworthy polac (an accident involving a police car) on Bedminster Down. I was subject to the usual sanction for bending a car: I was grounded and had to do foot patrol. I remained grounded until a retest was arranged, and my examiner was Sergeant Len Oatley. The drive I gave him was obviously good and successful and I was reinstated as a driver. The real mystery or surprise came shortly after, little more than a couple of months, when I was given a transfer to the Traffic Department. They say that if you drop in the mire, it helps. I do not know the name of the young lady, but she was certainly of great help, accelerating my transfer to the Traffic Department!

The move came in September 1970, so I had only achieved a little over four years' service. I suppose I could qualify as a 'flyer' as far as specialisation was concerned at that time. I joined the likes of John Bragg, John Ireland and Tim Dow, who were PCs, and Roger Britton, a sergeant. They all moved on up the rank structure, for those who might be reading this and recognise the names.

Animal Magic

Because of the nature of the job on Traffic, it takes you away from front-line pavement policing, and as much as I loved my twenty-four years on the division, there are not a lot of real stories to recount.

One of the funniest incidents I recall featured PC Paul Hodge, a dog and a speeding motorist. The collection of stray dogs from Bristol police stations was a daily task for the Traffic Department, carried out in the evening. The officer concerned was supposed to carry out the task with a van, a battered old Bedford van. Why would you want to get out of a sleek, sexy Triumph 2.5PI and use a van? The dogs were then taken to Bristol Dogs Home on Albert Road, Totterdown. However, on this particular evening Paul and I only had one dog to collect from Kingsweston Station and decided to do it in the car. I was driving, and on arrival at the station Paul went to get the dog while I turned the car around. Paul returned with the dog, which was not particularly big, and started off by putting it on the back seat. This is where it stayed until Paul called it onto his lap just after we set off. As dogs do, it did a couple of turns and then settled down for the journey and fell asleep. As we entered Hotwell Road from Dowry Square, I noticed a car being driven at high speed into Merchants Road. Deciding that it was worth a stop, I set off in hot pursuit onto the dual carriageway of the Cumberland System, an elevated road system over the city docks. It was well in excess of the speed limit, and as it weaved from lane to lane, so we had to do likewise, the cars rocking from side to side. As we approached the Long Ashton Bypass, I sounded the horns, put on the blue lights and pulled in ahead of the offender. Upon checking the mirror, I saw the errant driver was slowing down. We stopped and the car driver also did. Once stopped, he left his vehicle and started to approach us. As he did so, there was a revolting retching sound from the dog as it deposited the contents of its stomach straight into Paul's lap. I think Paul muttered something or other but the offender had reached our car just as Paul, legs wide apart, was climbing out. 'Is there a problem?' asked the offender. Paul replied, 'If we hadn't just had an accident, you would be reported.' The offender was allowed to go on his way while we beat a hasty retreat to the dogs' home to hand over the animal and wash the car mats, together with Paul's trousers. I then had to drive him home in his underpants to get clean trousers, the hope being, of course, that we would not be flagged down by a member of the public. Perhaps nowadays, in this liberal society, two policemen in a car, one without his trousers, would be accepted, but back then it would have been newspaper headlines, I am sure. Thankfully, luck was on our side and we were neither stopped by a member of the public nor indeed sent on a call.

It was not the last time that a patrol car was used for the carriage of animals. I was called to the Cribbs Causeway roundabout early one Sunday morning, where a stray goat had been seen. Sure enough, it was there, and very friendly but quite large. This was different to the German Shepherd dog that was guarding the nearby house when I went to knock and ask if they had lost a goat. I wisely stopped at the gate, so no enquiry was made there. Telephone calls to the zoo, the RSPCA and the dogs' home were all negative. So it was, that we decided, after some lateral thought, that the Mounted and Dog Section at their relatively new premises at Bower Ashton would provide a temporary home. But how to get it there was the challenge. Should we tie it to the rear bumper with a piece of string? But how fast does a goat run? And if it fell out of step, it could all become a bit messy! While we were there, my colleague had been feeding the goat the odd peppermint. This provided the answer. I drove the car up onto the grass and we opened the back doors. My colleague got into the back and offered the goat a peppermint and it came to the car to take it. My colleague then moved back a little and offered another one, and now the goat had to put its front hooves onto the rear seat. Man with peppermint then exited the car but offered another sweet, and the goat had to jump up onto the seat with all four legs to get it, then man with the peppermint slammed the doors. Success! It is amazing, the surprised looks you get on a Sunday morning when your rear seat passenger is a very large goat. No kidding! We conveyed it to the Mounted and Dog Section building, where we tied it to a hitching ring and drove quietly away. I never heard what happened thereafter! Different world. Arguably, a better world.

My kingdom for a horse

Animals featured in my life again while on the Traffic Department. When still a cadet, I had, together with my fellow cadets, been involved in creating nuisances to help train the police horses and so had a soft spot for the Mounted Section.

I thought it would be a good idea to seek a three-month equestrian course at the Mounted Section, an odd choice you might think, one specialist department to another, but I believe it was the opportunity to indulge in the 'pomp and ceremony' that the section has to offer. However, that was to be after the training.

I have to say that I had never ridden a horse; I knew which end was which, but that was as far as it went. I went down to the course with a degree of trepidation and the instructor, Sergeant Frank Knight, a lovely man, said, 'Look, chaps, there is nothing to worry about. If you work hard, listen to me and do what I tell you, then at the end of the course you will be jumping the low brush hurdles with no saddle, no reins and no stirrups.'

Yeah, I bet was my unspoken response, but nevertheless we worked hard, listened to Frank and did what he told us; and sure enough at the end of the course we were, as predicted, going over the brush hurdles with no saddle, no reins and no stirrups. Sometimes, just sometimes however, the horse did not come as well! But that's life!

Frank Knight was a real gentleman and Gary White was my fellow pupil. Our mounts were Redcliffe, a much-celebrated National Police Horse of the Year for a number of years on the trot at the Horse of the Year Show. He was also an absolute joy to ride.

It was like sitting in a comfortable easy chair and Redcliffe was so good at taking whatever aid you gave; a touch of the rein on the neck and we would change course, a touch – and I mean a touch – of the spur on his flanks and his rear end would start to come around.

Now, in my naivety I assumed a horse was a horse was a horse. Not so. The other horse, George, was, as I understood it, named after a previous chief constable, George Twist. I never paid too much attention to the way George Twist walked, but George the horse had the most ungainly and uncomfortable gait you could ever wish for. A most stubborn and uncomfortable mount. I was sweating profusely one day, trying to make him work, when Sergeant Knight shouted at me, 'Take him across to the bush!' I wondered to myself whether horses cocked their legs to relieve themselves, so when I eventually got to the bush, I braced myself just in case! 'Break a piece off the bush,' said Sergeant Knight, which I did. 'Now hit him with it!' shouted the sergeant, which I did. And all of a sudden George's ears were up and he was eager to do everything I wanted him to do. The following day, I was on George again, and as before he was lethargic and making no effort, so eventually I saw the bush coming around and fought to steer him towards it to grab another bit of branch, but as we got nearer, George obviously realised where we were heading and up came his ears and, once again, we were off and ready to work!

I never believed it was possible to ache in so many places at once. As time went on, though, I came to love the experience of riding, the feeling of being as one with the horse.

The nice side of the job was well balanced with the hard work of mucking out and cleaning and shining tack. There was a high standard to reach, a standard set by long-serving officers such as Alan Milsom, Jim Marment and Nobby Clarke, to name but a few. The Bristol, and then the Avon and Somerset, Mounted Section have long been a well-respected team both locally and nationally. The section is

Me and 'my' horse Redcliffe.

at times maligned by serving operational officers, but it provides a valuable PR arm to the job and in addition is still much needed when it comes to public disorder, major public events or searches of open land. Long may they continue.

However, I was not destined to continue with it. At the end of the course there was a written and practical exam. I had higher marks on the practical riding test, but Gary had higher marks on the theory, giving him a better aggregate mark. And so it was that the horse and I parted company; more comfortably, it has to be said, than when the hurdles were involved.

It was back to the Traffic Department.

My Bigger Job

Probably the best job I have ever been involved in was on nights as the Traffic Department A Division crime car, teamed with Tim Newman, then of A Division. Every night, A Division had to provide an officer to crew the so-called 'crime car'. The nice part was that the Traffic driver drove throughout the shift. Not everyone liked this, so I was always happy to do the crime car because it meant I could drive all night and enjoy the buzz of the drive on a 'shout'.

It was early morning, pretty dead, and as with most of these things, we were off our ground, riding through Bedminster, going back to A Division. As we came to the London Inn traffic lights at East Street we had to stop. It was then that I noticed an unlit

Vauxhall car coming towards us from the direction of the city. As it was passing us, the driver missed a gear and my attention was attracted to him. I noticed a big heap in the rear seat and another man sitting on the heap. I immediately turned about to stop the car. We then had a very short pursuit into a couple of back streets. As we rounded the final corner, we saw the car rolling forwards into a post, two men running from it and a third in the rear seat. The two men running were frantically pulling off stocking masks – not your run-of-the-mill happening in real life.

We drove after them as they ran towards a pedestrian lane. As we approached the lane, one of them, by *his* misfortune and *our* good fortune, changed direction and ran across the front of the car, so close that thankfully I could not avoid striking him and knocking him into a wall – unfortunately, not hard enough. He got up and again started running. We left the car and I gave chase to the two while Tim went to the car to detain the rear-seat man. My two split and I went after the one who had hit the wall, hoping he might be somewhat dazed. I caught him after a short distance and started to walk him back, but I could feel him resisting and I expected something to happen. It did. He became extremely violent and, despite having my truncheon in my hand, I could not manage to strike him anywhere that would hurt him enough to my benefit. We both went down. *I* was determined not to let go; *he* was determined to make me. It was the first time in my service I was really afraid. He was banging my head on the ground and I was shouting for Tim. As it was happening, I could imagine being left in a pool of blood. Fortunately, Tim came running and we managed to arrest him.

It transpired that they had been part of a gang that had hijacked a high-security cigarette delivery lorry. They had violently dragged the driver from his cab and were taking him away in the car; he was the 'heap' in the back. The other villains had driven the lorry away. A total of £42,000 worth of stock had been stolen. In those days that was a high-value load.

They had also stolen a van to offload the cigarettes into. This van had been secreted in an old colliery yard near Pensford, and it was to there that they drove the lorry. It all went wrong when the lorry became jammed in the entrance to the colliery and could not be moved in or out, thus trapping the getaway vehicle inside. Thankfully, with the exception of a couple of boxes of cigarettes that they could carry, the full load was recovered.

My man, who refused to name his colleagues in crime, was later sentenced to, as I recall, eight years' imprisonment. Sadly, the driver of the lorry, not a young man, had taken quite a beating. A few years later was admitted into Keynsham Hospital, where only a short time later he died. I have no doubt that the significant beating shortened his life.

Criminal Investigation Department (CID)

Under the Bristol Constabulary CID, attachments occurred every three months, with each territorial division supplying two officers plus a woman from W Division, and the Traffic Department supplied a further officer. At the start of the course, and in the classroom with others, the Detective Inspector made reference to my 'big job' and could not understand why I had not been given a commendation for the arrest. I appreciated his remarks.

As with many things in the job, reason did not seem to come into it; this course was no different. There was a slot for a Traffic man, and the fact that there was no such officer interested had no bearing; a pressed man would do, despite territorial officers queuing up for an attachment.

So it was that I began the worst six weeks of my career. The CID was, in those days, a different world to the rest of the job, or perhaps little has changed. I do not know; I would hope it has changed. You either worked an early shift, starting, as I recall, at 7 am or a split shift which, again as I recall, started at 10 am and finished at 2 pm and then you came back at, I think, 7 pm until 11 pm. When I turned up on the second half of the split shift I usually grabbed a fistful of crime reports to conduct follow-up enquiries, arriving back in the office perhaps by 8.30 pm, only to find that the other three officers had disappeared and, despite a search of the station, could not be found. However, as I said, it was a different world then and my understanding was that they would spend the remainder of their shift in a bar somewhere, 'gathering information', as you do! My answer to that was merely to disappear home, because if *they* could be paid for being in a pub for a few hours, then *I* could be paid for being at home.

I said that it was the worst six weeks, not three months, because after six weeks I went to Detective Inspector Davey Greenhough and told him of my discontent with the attachment. His question was, 'Well, why did you ask for the attachment?' He found it hard to understand when I told him that I had not requested the attachment and had indeed fought hard against it. It seemed even harder for him to understand that I had actually asked not to come but had still been sent. Within two days I was back on Traffic and much relieved.

The Amalgamation

In my opinion, 1 April 1974 was a major milestone for policing in Bristol. Sadly, Bristol lost its City and County status but from a Traffic Policing point of view and in relation to the Traffic Department it was like a breath of fresh air. Suddenly, Traffic cars began to carry necessary accident equipment in the car boot. I make this point because under Bristol, Traffic cars never carried any such necessities. If you were sent to a major accident and found that when you got there you needed signs, etc., you returned to the department and collected a large black wooden box that contained such items. That's efficiency for you. Not sure I ever bothered.

It was great having the big cars and the freedom but there were one or two certain officers who really did little in the way of traffic enforcement or arrests. Others were hard-working officers. John Ireland and John Bragg, who I mentioned earlier, were certainly two of the hard-working officers.

Wolseley 6/110 RE patrol

The only time Bristol came close to looking like a real Traffic Department, in my opinion, was as a result of the Regional Experiment (RE), where forces had to have patrol cars on major routes and those cars had to be white in colour, so one or two in Bristol had to be sprayed white to cover the usual black (see above). The car was normally single crewed, which suited me because I could work as hard as I wished without any negative influence. We had to wear a white-top cover to our caps and, as I recall, also white arm cuffs. I think the aim was to reduce casualties by always having a highly visible police car or motorcycle on the major routes. Some forty years on there is no chance of ever seeing a Traffic car on any route, it seems.

With the amalgamation of the forces and under the leadership of Chief Superintendent John Hughes, my chosen division very rapidly developed into a very professional body. Vehicles became far better and far newer. I had my first encounter with the Triumph 2.5PI. In my humble opinion, this vehicle has never been bettered as the ideal police patrol car. Well, certainly not in my time.

It was interesting and good fun to be part of the Road Traffic Department, renamed the Road Motor Patrol. When I started on Traffic we were based at New Bridewell in the heart of the city, and one evening on my way into a night shift, and much to my embarrassment, my Ford Cortina ran out of petrol on the A4 at Brislington, near Eagle Road. That night I was driving the patrol car for the A Division crime car and was teamed with a non-driver from A Division. During the first half of the shift I collected a gallon of petrol from Temple Meads Motors (no longer there) and drove out to my car and put the fuel in. During the refreshment break I spoke to Fred (another PC) and he agreed to bring my blue Cortina back to the station. At the end of my shift I drove into Nelson Street, but no sign of my Cortina. There was, however, another one, which was green. I spoke to Fred, who told me he had collected it and parked it in Nelson Street. 'What colour was it?' I asked, and he replied, 'Green!' Fords were infamous for one key fitting all, so Fred had to describe as best he could where he had 'collected' this other car from, and I, with a police escort, did my best to park it back where I thought it might have been parked earlier. Nothing was ever reported, so presumably the owner questioned his own memory that morning.

The Stolen Minibus

Sunday mornings were often very quiet, but at about 11.30 am on this particular Sunday, I was driving and Larry Andrews was the observer when we received a circulation regarding a stolen minibus. Now, just occasionally fate and luck will fall your way, and as we drove along Bedminster Down on the A38, there ahead was the very minibus. We closed on it and put the blues on and flashed the headlights, hoping that the driver would just give up. Wishful thinking!

The situation was compounded by a sponsored cycle ride on the same road, and it was terrifying following the vehicle and seeing ahead of it groups of cyclists, which the driver seemed to aim for, and all you could do was sit and wait to see bodies coming from under the vehicle. Thankfully, he seemed to manage to veer out at the last minute each time. This continued until we reached Churchill, where the driver decided to turn right towards Congresbury, a much narrower road where we could do nothing to stop him, but still there were pockets of cyclists from the ride, we presumed heading for Weston-super-Mare. As we came into Congresbury I told Larry to get on the radio and ask for permission to ram the vehicle. Our commentary had been continuous on the radio, so no one was in any doubt about our predicament. After a while the response from the duty inspector came back: 'Do what you have to!' I am not sure that was categorically permission to ram, but clearly we had to stop him. By now we had followed the minibus onto the A370, heading for Weston-super-Mare. We heard over the radio that Traffic cars had stopped vehicles in the other direction from coming towards us, so the moment we had the opportunity, we drew alongside the vehicle and Larry leant out the window, calling for the driver to stop. He was not interested, so I told Larry to get himself fully back in the car, which he did. I then drove slightly faster until the front half of my car was ahead of the minibus and then quickly turned the steering wheel to the left, enough that the side of the car impacted the front of the vehicle but I had swiftly steered ahead again. The contact sent the minibus veering to the nearside, where it collided with a roadside pole carrying power cables. We were quickly out of the vehicle and into the back of the minibus to grab the driver and drag him out. He turned out to be only sixteen and was arrested by Larry. The good fortune was that the only damage to the patrol car was a dent in the rear nearside passenger door, so not a great cost. The poor fortune was that the pole carrying the power cables had been sufficiently damaged that we deprived Hewish of their Sunday lunch if their cookers were electric!

Margaret Thatcher

There was another time I managed to make contact with another vehicle when driving a patrol car. It was when Margaret Thatcher MP was seeking the top job. She was Conservative Party leader coming into a general election. She had stayed the night in a hotel on Redcliffe Way and her 'battle bus' coach was in the car park; it was being given a motorcycle escort to the next engagement just beyond the top of Park Street in Bristol. I was driving the follow car with the superintendent on board in the front passenger seat. However, we were parked in the car park of a building, I believe belonging to St Mary Redcliffe Church, and we were to drive out and drop in behind the coach via Pump Lane. I do not fully recollect how or why the coach got away so swiftly but I drove to the exit of the car park where we were. There were parked cars on both sides of the exit and on both sides of the road. I looked left. It was clear. Then I looked right, having to do this through the nearest vehicle, which was white, and through to the far side of the road to another white car, and it was clear. Or so I had thought! Sadly, between the two white cars was another white car, and while I had not properly registered it, it was moving, and as I swung out, there it was. Sadly, there was a collision. I reversed back into the car park and the other car followed, facing me. The superintendent was out and running to get into another car and I was left there. It took a while to realise that the superintendent had not summoned a supervisory to deal with the polac. I quickly corrected this and the sergeant arrived. There was every chance I was going to be grounded and indeed reported for driving without due care and attention. However, a few days later a letter arrived at the Avon Street Traffic Centre that seemed to be of a help to me. I cannot claim friends in high places, but here was the lady who promised to do good things for police pay if she was elected. Not surprisingly, she got my vote.

From

The Rt. Hon. Mrs Margaret Thatcher

Conservative & Unionist Central Office, 32 Smith Square, Westminster SW1P 3HH

19th April 1979

Dear Constable Hale,

I am just writing to say how sorry I was about the accident you had on Tuesday. I know from my own Detectives that there was the possibility of a demonstration outside the BBC Buildings in Bristol and that it was therefore felt that a reserve police car should follow my own car to the Studios. I am sorry that in the hasty departure from the Dragonara Hotel this accident occurred and I much appreciate what you were trying to do to help. I do hope that there will be no unfortunate repercussions over this accident.

With best wishes.

Yours sincerely

Margaret Thatcher

P C Hale

Two Memorable Fast Runs

The two runs were memorable but for different reasons. The longest was one morning when I was instructed to return to New Bridewell and collect the communications inspector and a set of listening-and-observation technical gear and take them to Dulverton Police Station on the edge of Exmoor, as they were dealing with a siege situation. At that time, the M5 was not completed, so we travelled down the A38 and onto other roads, a journey of some 65 miles, which we accomplished in about ninety minutes, as we had the use of blue lights and two-tone horns. The latter were the subject of some disagreement in the car, as I would leave them on to warn traffic ahead and the inspector would turn them off, causing me to turn them on; eventually he gave up. I was using a Triumph 2.5, but not the PI, and when we eventually drew up at Dulverton Police Station, you could have been forgiven for thinking the car was on fire because of the copious smoke coming from the brakes. A great journey to have had the opportunity to drive.

The other memorable fast run was sadly for an extremely traumatic reason. On 10 April 1973 some 140 people, mainly mothers, boarded Invicta Airlines Flight 435 at Bristol Airport, happily looking forward to a day's shopping and sightseeing in Basle. It was the third annual outing for members of Axbridge Ladies Guild, joined on this occasion by women from the Cheddar Mums' Night Out group, skittles players from Wrington and Congresbury, plus friends and relatives. Travelling with one of these groups was the wife of a Bristol policeman. When the plane struck the tops of trees and crashed into a hillside on its second attempt to land at the Swiss airport during a snowstorm, 108 people were killed.

Before the final extent of the tragedy was known, a flight was arranged for relatives to go out that afternoon. The policeman whose wife was involved, who unbeknown to us had in fact died, did not have a passport, so I had to collect him, I think from duty, take him to his home to get the necessary papers and then take him to the Passport Office, which was fortunately then in Bristol. They pulled out all the stops and he was given a passport in double-quick time. I then had to rush him out to Bristol Airport to be able to take the flight. All of this was achieved on blue lights and two-tone horns. When it was one of its own, the police service was at that time outstanding in making things happen. I truly hope the situation is the same nowadays.

The Motorcycle Section

When I returned from the Mounted Section equestrian course, I decided I wanted to work solo, and the best way to achieve this was to become a member of the Motorcycle Section. This I managed to achieve, and life was good. It was around about 1979/80 that I became a Traffic motorcyclist based in Bristol. Much of our work was to deal with road hold-ups and obstructions, but by the same token we also got involved in other matters, including crime.

Write the wrong number down

As a motorcyclist you had a bit of a free-ranging remit, and that meant you could respond to jobs when you heard them. For a large proportion of the time, though, you were able to deal with those breaking the traffic law – some major, some minor. Breaching single- and double-yellow lines was widespread, and one afternoon on Gloucester Road, the main A38, I found a whole line-up of cars on yellow lines. I parked the bike at the head of the queue and started working my way down, writing tickets and sticking them on the windscreens. Many drivers returned, took the tickets and drove off. I was dealing with the last two when I saw a car pull up just up the road from my machine, so I noted the time and registration number. I completed the last two tickets and slowly walked up to the latest arrival, writing the ticket as I approached. I reached the car and after a minute or so a young guy came running over shouting for me to hang on, saying he was a policeman and on duty. The police can park on yellows for police purposes. He told me he was from Redland CID, so I asked why he had not come down to me and explained the situation on arrival. He had no answer. I said to him, 'Sorry, but you will have to sort the matter out with your sergeant and if the ticket is quashed, then so be it.'

Then he said, 'Can you write the wrong car registration number on the ticket so it will bounce?'

Somewhat shocked, I replied, 'I do not believe I am hearing this, but if you say anything else, I shall arrest you for attempting to pervert the course of justice. It frightens me that if you can ask me to do that, what lies do you tell in the witness box?'

He received his ticket and I expect paid it!

The machete

Sometimes things happen out of the blue that are a bit more tasty than fixed-penalty tickets. On 29 April 1986, on the Bath Road, just after lunchtime and on my way to work on my personal motorcycle but in full uniform motorcycle gear, a car did a U-turn in front of me, and because of the manner in which it was done, I came up behind him and stopped him. I came alongside, and as I looked into the car, he reached to the nearside footwell and picked up a machete saying, 'Right then, let's sort this out.'

I said, 'Don't be stupid. Put it down.'

He then got out of his vehicle, pointing the machete at me in a threatening manner. I pulled my machine back and he shouted, 'I've had enough of this aggro. Let's get the law.'

He moved towards me, still holding the machete. I drove my

motorcycle around him and down the road some 15 metres. I then stopped the first car that approached and asked the driver to ring the police on 999 to report where I was and that I needed assistance. I then went towards the driver, and as I did so, he put the machete back in the car. I closed with him and took hold of his arm and told him he was being arrested for having an offensive weapon. I put him in handcuffs. His reply was, 'I thought it was someone going to grab me and I had it in there from earlier. I didn't realise you were a policeman.'

Later that day
The day did not end there, because during the rush hour, as the result of a radio circulation, I stopped a Rover motor car driven by a criminal and carrying another criminal. I was joined by another motorcycle colleague and a territorial divisional officer. The driver agreed to a search of the car, but while we were engaged in that, the passenger wandered off. My motorcycle colleague, who for some reason was not too switched on, never stopped him but pointed to where he had gone. I went into the nearby depot, where the divisional officer was already with the passenger. I noticed he had something in his hand.

Upon being asked what he had, he tried to run and a struggle ensued. He managed to move to a doorway and throw two containers to the driver. One was caught by the other motorcyclist, and the driver caught the other one and threw it over the roof of the building. The passenger put up a struggle with me while my motorcycle colleague stood doing nothing, only watching. 'Have you got handcuffs?' I shouted.

'Yes' was the answer.

'Well, for goodness sake, get them out and put them on him.' There were those colleagues I sometimes wondered about!

Once he was cuffed, he was held by my motorcycle colleague and the divisional officer. I then saw the driver struggling violently with another officer. I ran to them, pocketbook in one hand and aware that the criminal had infectious hepatitis, so the easiest way was to kick him extremely hard on his leg – proportionate force. Success. He stopped fighting. He was also cuffed and both were arrested by the divisional officers.

That same evening, I had to settle down and give a driving talk to members of the public on a 'Towards Better Motoring' course, a good example of the breadth of action required of a police officer, making no two days the same!

How did you know it was nicked?

On another occasion during the evening rush hour, I was parked on my motorcycle monitoring traffic, when out of a nearby junction came a car with two young males inside. I noticed that the quarter-light window on the driver's side had been smashed, so there was every chance the car was stolen. Most cars of that time had a small hinged window in front of the main front-door side windows. By smashing this small window, you could then put your hand in and unlock the door. The very moment I put the bike into gear, they drove away at high speed towards Temple Meads Railway Station, with me in pursuit. They turned left up the railway incline approach road and then into a car park in the old Brunel platform before driving outside into a dead end. They came to a quick stop and the driver ran one way while the passenger ran the other and reached a chain link fence, seemingly wanting to climb it. Fortunately, I was still on the motorcycle and rode towards him but started to skid forward due to braking on the chipping surface! He was next to a concrete fence post and at the right moment had his legs apart. It is amazing how having your genitals caught between a concrete fence post and the front wheel of a large BMW motorcycle convinces you to give up. He was arrested. When arrested, his claim was, 'I was forced into the car and told to keep my mouth shut, then I was told to run.'

At this time we had a police helicopter on trial and it came overhead to keep watch on a nearby derelict site where the driver had run to, containing it while some other officers closed in. Driver arrested. Later at the station the driver saw me and said, 'You the copper on the bike?'

'Yes,' I said.

'How did you know we nicked the car?'

In response, I shrugged, and he asked 'What, was it just a routine check?' Obviously, he never noticed a copper's nose!

Dynamic Risk Assessment

There are times you might have to do something different. Just before lunch one day, I was on motorcycle patrol in the Bristol city centre when the call came over that a car had gone into the city's floating harbour almost opposite the SS *Great Britain*. I said I would attend and was there within a few minutes. When I arrived, there was a small crowd and a man standing on a boat in the water. He was soaking wet and saying his wife was still in the car. There was no sign of the car, nor indeed air bubbles. I then had a decision to make. I asked whether anyone was local, and a few said they were. My next question was, 'How deep?' The answer came back that it was probably some 20 feet. This, of course, was a stretch of water that had catered for large merchant ships at one time. My final question was, 'How long has it been in there?', and the answer to that question was, 'At least five minutes.' I decided that there was no chance of me achieving a rescue and no point in going in. Today they would call that a dynamic risk assessment. A very short time later the fire appliance arrived and the crew stripped down to their pants and leapt in, all returning to the surface saying to their leading hand that they could not see anything because it was black and they could not reach the bottom. Yes, good decision. Dry! Sad as it was, there was nothing that could be achieved. A while later a police task force unit arrived and one of the crew was part of the Underwater Search Unit. He borrowed a breathing apparatus from the fire service, and thus equipped, he went in and managed to find the car and retrieve the body.

Some years later, while a member of Keynsham Lions Club, we used to have monthly dinner meetings with a guest speaker. I had invited the sergeant in charge of the Underwater Search Unit to speak, and over dinner I related the incident to him. I asked his opinion and said that I had never had a guilty conscience about my decision not to try to find her. His response was that had I gone in in the attendant circumstances, and he had seen me, I would have been the recipient of a good rollicking. He also said that the policeman who had gone in with a borrowed non-regulation diving breathing apparatus got an even bigger rollicking!

The Clifton Suspension Bridge

Ambulance escorts were often undertaken by the motorcyclists. The reason for these escorts was to get people to hospital to try to save their lives. However, from the perspective of the motorcyclist – well, certainly me – they were a great buzz. From time to time we would be sent to Portbury Roundabout on the M5 to await the arrival of an ambulance from deepest Cornwall bearing a mum who had not long given birth and her newborn infant in an incubator. The ambulances were bound for Bristol Children's Hospital. I always felt sorry for the mums because just a relatively short time after the trauma of childbirth they were whisked hundreds of miles away, often with Dad in the family car, headlights on, trying to keep up with the ambulance. The route from the M5 to the hospital took us over the world-famous Clifton Suspension Bridge. At each entry they have a toll barrier, and as the motorcycle approached with twos and blues, the bridge keepers would lift the barrier mechanically and through would go the escorts, but the keepers seemed not to have a system to keep the barrier up and it would then come down, only to be destroyed by a speeding ambulance. Thankfully, the barriers were made of plastic.

One Sunday evening, on the way home from my equestrian course, I was delivering some Avon products for Jane, who was for a while an Avon lady, to a customer in Clifton. My route from the stables took me over the suspension bridge, and as I approached the Bristol end of the bridge I became aware of a man climbing the railings to jump. Speed was of the essence as I jerked on the handbrake while opening my door and running. I managed to get to him before he had completed his climb. I grabbed hold of him but he put up some resistance. Fortunately, the man in the car behind had seen what was happening and also came across. Together we pulled him down. It seems that he was separated from his family and only saw his children at the weekends, but not every weekend. I handed him over to another police unit that had been called by the bridge keepers and went on my way.

Helicopter landing marshal

Sometimes as a motorcyclist you ended up working with a helicopter, either with the arrival of royals or perhaps a medical evacuation into the centre of Bristol, with the aircraft landing on College Green. It was decided that a few people should be trained as helicopter landing marshals just in case.

So it was, that three of us attended Yeovilton Royal Naval Air Service base. During the morning, we were given a safety briefing, a talk by the station fire service, and instruction on how to exit a helicopter that had ditched into water. The one thing I remember from the last part was 'always follow the bubbles' – very important because they are heading for the surface!

We were then treated to a nice meal, and after that we were split up because, as I recall, the inspector was taken to the officers' mess while the sergeant and I were taken to the sergeants' mess. Know your place in life! I suppose I was lucky to make the sergeants'

One of the joys of the motorcycle section was escorts of all types, and here I had been part of the escort for The Duchess of York, Sarah Ferguson. I am the far end, next to me is Richard 'Magic' Wand, then Dave 'Cordite' Corden, followed by Roger 'Crusher' Cave and finally the eccentric but 'lovable' Sergeant Steve 'Scotty' Scott.

mess. As we were heading in, I told our host that I was calling into the lavatory. When I came back and joined them in the bar, he had bought me a pint of beer. Now, I am not, and never have been, a beer drinker, or indeed any other intoxicants, save for the odd glass of wine. Sensibly, I should have declined the drink, but not wanting to offend anyone, I foolishly took the beer and really struggled through the process of drinking it.

We then went out to the helicopter. At this point it has to be said that I had never flown before, but in I got into the rear of the Westland Whirlwind – I think that's what it was – and settled down for the flight. The big side door was open and I was sitting to one side of it trying to enjoy the view. 'Come over here,' called the crewman from the opposite side. Well, that was a leap of faith hoping the craft did not decide to lean into a right-hand turn before

I was seated and belted. However, the view was fantastic. We landed once or twice so that turns could be taken to sit beside the pilot. I think I was second up, and perhaps it was during this time that my stomach started to feel unsettled. By the time we were coming into land I was in the rear, and as we touched down and started to taxi along the runway, I was hanging out of the side door spreading the contents of my stomach as we went, including lunch and the culprit . . . the pint of beer.

In the evening we were given another meal; however, I ate very little of it. We were due to have a night flight and I was concerned the same thing might happen again. Advice was to drink plenty of lemonade, which I did, and the flight was fine.

After the training, I marshalled a few royal visit testing flights, where they come in to ensure that on the day it is all going to be fine. It was interesting on one such exercise standing at the landing site at Barton Hill in Bristol and searching the sky for the approaching dot, seeing it and standing out ready, to be told after they had landed that, thanks to my hi-vis cuffs, they had spotted me from some 12 miles out.

The Siege at Keynsham

Early on in our married life, Jane and I had rented a flat in Broadlands House, St. Francis Road, Keynsham, but by a date that escapes me – but post 1970, or perhaps post 1974 – we were living in a council house in St John's Court, Keynsham. It was there, very early one morning, that I was contacted by a PC and asked to attend Keynsham Police Station with all haste. Upon my arrival I walked into a large gathering of officers awaiting briefing. It was thought that an IRA terrorist team were holed up in the Broadlands Farmhouse, next to Broadlands House, and I was there to provide 'expert advice' on the layout of the area. I was good for something then!

After the briefing, we all made our way to our respective positions. Somehow or other, I was as front line as front line can be. Together with the detective chief inspector from Bath, I was secreted behind a gatepost at the end of the drive, looking up at this house, which was unlived in, and watching for any sign of movement. It was a cold morning, so any shivering could be put down more to temperature than fear.

Between the house and the gatepost was a small, somewhat tatty, apparently derelict caravan. Suddenly, it dawned on us that this mobile shelter might contain the suspected persons. We decided that perhaps we should check it; with hindsight, perhaps not a sensible idea. In the best SAS style, the chief inspector and I closed on the caravan and once there took the bull by the horns and levered up a piece of board covering one of the windows. You will gather that, as I am able to relate this story in print, no one was inside.

It was then decided by those in charge that a closer look at the house itself was needed. So it was, that the then, I believe, inspector or chief inspector at Keynsham, John Masters, appeared on the horizon dressed in a postman's uniform and riding a red post office pedal cycle. There were those who spoke humorously of 'typecasting', as you might imagine.

Once the 'postman' had called, a decision was made to move in on the building. Looking back down the road, I could see the assault team, headed by Leslie Pearce, the then deputy chief constable, smartly dressed in his overcoat and backed by an assortment of uniformed and plain-clothed officers, plus one or two dog handlers and the odd firearms officer. They were marching two or three abreast up to the road. Clearly, no thoughts about a covert approach – more a parade, but without a flag! So it was, that I joined that parade.

When we reached the house, entry was forcibly affected, and much to my surprise, and not a little excitement, I found myself fourth through the door, behind a dog handler, a couple of officers with guns and one other. Needless to say, the house was empty. I often wonder what might have happened had it not been. The pleasures of old-style policing. No risk assessment; just get on with doing the job. Who needs body armour and tactical firearms teams! How things have changed – some for the good but much for the worse. Good times. Arguably, better times.

This was during the Troubles, and active cells of the IRA terrorist organisation were working here on the mainland, placing bombs to kill and maim. One evening, while on late tour, a report came in that a bomb had been placed in Park Street, Bristol, and my crewmate and I were sent to close the road at College Green. We could see fire engines plus their crew, and also police officers, at the top end of Park Street. We had been there a little while when we heard a massive explosion near a parked fire engine. As I recall, the engine protected most if not all from the blast. However, the frightening thing to me was the knowledge that it was the IRA's practice to have one bomb as a 'come-on' to bring the uniformed services to the location and then a second bomb planted where people would likely be evacuated to. So for some while we maintained our position on the road closure but wondered whether we were close to, or too close to, that second bomb. Thankfully, this tactic had not been used that evening.

Police Federation

In the latter months of 1975, PC Brian McDowell (who sadly passed away in 2019) decided that he no longer wished to be the constables' representative for the Traffic Department on the Joint Branch Board of the Police Federation (the police union, but without the power to take strike action). Thus, an election was called. The fight was between me and a PC from Taunton. At that time Almondsbury Motorway Unit, which had been part of the

Gloucestershire Constabulary, was akin to Broadbury Road and its officers in that it had not accepted amalgamation. Donald Duck could have stood against the man from Taunton and won because the vote from Bristol and Almondsbury undoubtedly would not have been cast for a 'county' man – rather sad, but I had to grasp whatever was going.

Thankfully, having won, I believe I worked positively for the force as a whole.

This was the beginning of thirteen very rewarding years as a Federation rep. The Police Federation is the staff association for the so-called rank and file, essentially chief inspectors and below. At times it was frustrating; being somewhat radical, I suppose I was a few years ahead of my time.

After a few years I became the secretary of the Constables Branch Board, a position I held until 1989. During those years I believe I played a positive role, achieving the issue of the anorak, or car coat, as an accepted part of the uniform. I also achieved the NATO sweater a few years later.

In particular for the Traffic Department, I was able to acquire a superior anorak to that of the general issue, and the old cap with an ill-fitting plastic cover was replaced by a much smarter cap with an integrated white top. Motorcyclists also gained by their original leathers being replaced with a far better product.

At the time of the miner's strike, the whole of the force, with the exception of Traffic and A Division, were earning large amounts of overtime at the coalfields. Recognising the injustice, I took the matter to the branch board and, after significant resistance, convinced them to approach the chief and negotiate for Traffic men to be able to form a Police Support Unit (PSU) together with A-Division men. This was achieved. I never accepted any opportunities to go, and indeed was offered the first joint PSU but declined it, believing that it would have seemed like the result of self-interest rather than having achieved it for the men.

During my thirteen years, I attended the national conference on eleven occasions and spoke at most, if not all. I became reserve to the regional representative on the national committee and reserve to the conference arrangements committee. I regularly attended national secretaries' meetings, and locally, as part of the executive committee, attended consultation meetings with the Association of Chief Police Officers (ACPO) and the Police Superintendents' Association. All of these forums provided a very practical opportunity to promote the interests of the Traffic Department, which I did at all opportunities over thirteen years.

Sadly, in 1989, at the December election, on the strength of a poster slogan that read 'Perhaps it's time for a change', just over half the division deserted me and everything I had tried to do for them. There we are. Democracy rules.

The Apple Appeal

Thankfully, the branch board allowed me to continue as the chairman of the 'Apple Appeal' committee. The Apple Appeal had been established some ten years earlier following a discussion between Inspector Paul Rabbeth, the Federation chairman, and myself about what we might be able to do for those Royal Ulster Constabulary officers who had been wounded, maimed or intimidated into leaving their homes by the IRA.

The outcome was that I became chairman of the appeal and we organised a full week-long holiday every year, here in Somerset, for four officers and their spouses. We flew them across to Bristol Airport, hired a minibus, which I drove, and lodged them in a hotel, ultimately in Keynsham. We then ran a week of outings, meals, and tours of Courage Brewery, which seemed to prove popular; it might have been the magnificent buffet they provided, but I think the free beer and gifts might have won the day.

We did a tour of both Bath and Bristol, and a lovely man called Bob Porton helped us as a guide in both city tours. When we went to Dulverton in deepest Somerset, on the Saturday, the police wives from this small station made loads of cake and provided tea and coffee for our elevenses. We then went on across Exmoor to Dunster, where at The Luttrell Arms we were treated to a three-course lunch by the manager, Mr Mann, another lovely man, who always had a gift arranged for each couple.

They were lovely occasions, and Jane would take leave every year to be with me and our guests throughout the week; other Federation officers would also dip in and out, together with their wives or husbands. For ten years we managed to raise funds to carry out this week of rest and relaxation for our colleagues from the RUC, but then sadly fundraising became a challenge. However, as one door closes on my Federation and road motor patrol days, another was soon to open that gave me a great end to my police service, of which more later.

Riots

St Pauls

Prior to April 1980 riots were not something that the people of Bristol had experienced in their living memory, or indeed their parents' memory. The St Pauls district of the city was soon to change all of that.

St Pauls had once been a good-class area close to the city centre and it had, indeed, been my home for the first ten years of my life. However, in the late 1950s and into the 1960s the white population gradually became displaced by a large Afro-Caribbean one. The area gradually became run down and little was spent on it to improve the quality of life of the community. It was a time when there was still a large division between white and black communities and derogatory names for blacks fell easily off the tongue, both in the population at large and indeed the police service.

Relationships between police and black communities were not good and often strained. There was a proportion of criminality within the black community, particularly within the younger generation, and putting that alongside a definite contempt for the law and the people that strove to uphold it within that generation, things could only go from bad to worse.

I had been to court on 2 April that year and it was late afternoon when I returned to the Avon Street Traffic Unit, where I was stationed. With a little of my shift left, I decided to go out on patrol. As I turned the patrol car radio on, I began to monitor many transmissions regarding major problems in Grosvenor Road, St Pauls, where a drugs raid had taken place at the infamous Black & White Café. Assistance was being called for. I ran back into the building and told Inspector Dave Heiron – sadly, no longer with us following an untimely death after retirement – what was happening and together we set off for Grosvenor Road. Arriving at the Inkerman Pub at the end of Grosvenor Road, the junction with Wilder Street, we joined a group of uniform officers, perhaps some twenty-strong.

The situation was bad, with a number of Drugs Squad officers trapped in the café. Clearly, we had to do something. We were called into three ranks – the benefit of a disciplined body – and were marched towards the café. As we came out from the cover of the pub and into the area of Grosvenor Road bounded by flats and a grassed area, we came under attack by a large presence of the black community. They threw everything they could find: bricks, bottles, stones – you name it, it was falling on us. This was something none of us had experienced in our careers as police officers. It was odd because, while it was dangerous, you were comforted by the knowledge that there was as much chance of another officer being struck as there was of you – or does that sound selfish? As we progressed, some men managed to pick up dustbin lids to use as shields.

Eventually, we arrived at the café and entered. The officers involved in the raid were safe and well. Having got in, we now had to get out again and move back to a position of relative safety. Many of us now upended crates of beer to avail ourselves of the crates as protection against the missiles. So, suitably equipped with personal beer crates and dustbin lids, out we went, yet again to be subjected to a bitter onslaught by the gathered community. Unscathed, I arrived back at the area of the Inkerman with all my colleagues.

So much had happened since the first radio message to the control room at 4.31 pm from those involved in the raid: a dog handler had been injured sufficiently to need an ambulance, his vehicle damaged by missiles, a police motorcyclist had been hit off his machine and the bus company had dialled 999 to report another PC needing assistance.

Very soon all available dog handlers were called to the area and various Traffic patrol cars attended, as did units from the other three Bristol divisions. Just after 5.15 pm shields were called for, but in those days they were stored centrally, not held on available vehicles. At about the same time, Avon Ambulance Service were alerted, to put them on standby, but they had only one unit available to keep for our needs. Just before 5.30 pm it was reported that two police cars had been set on fire and the fire brigade attended.

At about this time, small support groups were put on standby. I mean small – three sergeants and twenty-three PCs from three divisions in the south. This was typical of the ability of the police service not to be able to respond in strength, or speed. It has changed a little, but not a lot. The police service is often a bluff; yes, you might put a large group of officers at an incident, but it is likely they have been drawn from other divisions, and those divisions are now patrolled by a skeleton staff.

Shortly after 5.30 pm the chief constable and deputy chief

constable, Messrs Weigh and Smith respectively, attended the general area. In my view this was the first command mistake. You do not want or need the supreme commander and deputy on or near the front line. Subordinate supervisors then seem reluctant to make operational decisions, looking over their shoulder in case the chief is there. One such situation, as I saw it, involved myself and others of the rank and file who were by now strung out along Grosvenor Road facing the opposing ranks in a stand-off. While so arranged, I saw at least one youth arriving behind the other line, the front of his jacket bulging and his arms supporting an obvious weight. As he stood there, I saw him emptying his load onto the ground: a large pile of big stones ready for throwing at us. I pointed this out to a superintendent who had been a 'county' man and was standing nearby, and I suggested we take action, but I was told not to worry myself about it. But surely isn't that what police officers do? They arrest criminals? Someone building up a stock of ammunition in a riot situation is a criminal.

We were only a few years beyond amalgamation, Bristol Constabulary with Somerset and Bath. It was my view that the style of policing adopted by the county force was very different from that of the city. As a city force, we would act very positively and firmly to quell disorder. The county style seemed to be somewhat opposed to that, perhaps because out in the county the nearest help might be miles away. Perhaps this was why the ex-'county' senior officer did not want to go in hard and fast.

At about 6.15 pm the number of officers either at the scene or on standby had still only reached into the seventies. There were rumours that units from the Metropolitan Police had been offered later that evening but had been turned down. The running joke was that they had been turned down because we did not need anyone killed yet. (Blair Peach, a New Zealand-born teacher, was allegedly killed by the actions of the Metropolitan Police Special Patrol Group at an anti-Nazi league demonstration in 1979.)

At about 6.30 pm the police breakdown truck arrived to remove one of the burnt-out police cars. I was asked to escort it to Trinity Road Police Station. Having hitched up the disabled car and started to move off, the truck came under attack and I radioed a priority message. At this time a sergeant dog handler came running along Grosvenor Road with his dog to try to help, but in the confusion the wreck that was under tow swung sideways, knocking him to the ground. Fortunately, other officers were around to ensure his safety. I believe he suffered damage to his legs. Once I had completed the escort task, I started to make my way back to the area.

By now some shields had been provided and officers were advancing down City Road but coming under sustained bombardment. While en route I monitored a radio message saying that urgent assistance was needed at the junction of City Road and Ashley Road. I responded – no one waits to be sent when a police officer calls for urgent assistance – and I drove up Sussex Place at speed, with horns and blue lights operating, carving a channel through the traffic. As I came within yards of the junction, I could see the back of a whole hoard of the black community throwing missiles into City Road, presumably towards the aforementioned shield units. However, upon hearing my approach, a dozen or so turned, saw me, broke away from the mob and ran towards me, throwing bricks and stones at my vehicle. It only took a split second on my part to decide that I had to get away, so with lights and horns still operating, I began reversing at great speed back through the traffic I had just come through. All of the time, I could hear missiles crashing into the vehicle, one such object smashing the windscreen. Once out of harm's way, I began to circumnavigate the area to reach what had been the RV (rendezvous) point at the Inkerman Pub.

However, the disorder continued and three police cars were now on fire. At around 7.15 pm the Traffic patrol cars were withdrawn and were to be used as back-up. At the same time, divisions were being asked to send all possible help and to leave only one vehicle to police each district. In other words, there were just eight police officers policing Bristol, other than at St Pauls.

Not long after, there came the second command decision by the chief constable that, in my view, was a very sad day for policing in Bristol; the chief constable withdrew police from St Pauls. This is when anarchy came to the streets and Lloyds Bank in Sussex Place, among other buildings, was burnt to the ground. The stupidity of it is unbelievable; why burn down your own community?

Not content with that, the cycle shop opposite was burgled and looted and there were reports of a shop in Brighton Street and a post office being broken into, as well as St Paul's Day Nursery being set on fire. Motorcycles were being stolen from Fowlers motorcycle shop. Mindless morons, because it was *their* community facilities they were destroying. Understandably, the fire brigade had to turn back from fires because the police were not attending to protect them. Later there were reports that all shops in Sussex Place were being looted.

As the evening wore on there were many calls from members of the public concerned for relatives living in St Pauls. There were also calls reporting the various crimes being committed. At just after 8.30 pm a man rang the police to say that there was a mob of some 500–700, mainly black, in Ashley Road.

By 8.45 pm personnel were en route to Bristol from the outer divisions and other forces. A while later a man from London rang to say that he could raise a force of civilians to come to Bristol to help the police. He was thanked for his offer but it was declined. He said he would ring later to see if we had changed our mind. One can only wonder how the course of history might have been changed. However, considering that the chief constable had withdrawn the police, the situation might not have been any worse.

A while later, units from Wiltshire were travelling to the city. The 'carnival' atmosphere continued in Sussex Place with some 300–400 youths milling around.

Throughout this time, the police received many calls from the public concerned for the welfare of people living in the area and did nothing about it. What a sadness and embarrassment. What was once a proud city force was not serving the public, who looked to it for protection. It was not maintaining the Queen's peace, something that every officer had sworn to do when they had joined. Decisions and leadership were now, it seemed, vested in the hands of officers more versed in the problems of the market town and rural areas.

Just before 11 pm officers from the Devon and Cornwall Constabulary were making their way to the city. Just before midnight a call was received by both the police and the *Western Daily Press* saying that 'coachloads of coloureds are coming from Birmingham armed to kill the police'. For the next two hours motorway patrols monitored the M5 between the two cities.

As the night wore on, things calmed down a little and surrounding forces were now in evidence on our streets. It was so sad that we relinquished the streets to the mob for so long. I cannot help but ponder how different it would have been had Ken Steele still been chief constable. Although he was a 'county' man, he was charismatic and a born leader.

It was perhaps a turning point in my career, because up until that day there was nowhere I would have been afraid to go. But suddenly I realised that the blue uniform is not, in fact, a suit of armour and that we were very vulnerable. It manifested itself that same night, because when I got back to the station after my car had been attacked, with me in it, I suddenly began to tremble uncontrollably – presumably, delayed shocked at how easily I could have been killed had the car stalled.

It was some time before matters returned to a degree of

normality in the area but it took Operation Delivery, sometime later, to reclaim the streets. Many hundreds of officers deluged the streets in a pre-planned surprise 'invasion'. They arrived in plain white hire vans and by the coachloads, one of which I was driving. It was hoped that large quantities of drugs would be found, but this did not happen. There was a rumour that those in the area who were up to no good were tipped off by a police sergeant. So sad if true.

Policing in St Pauls would never be the same again.

Hartcliffe Riot

It was just over twelve years later, in July 1992, when some people in Hartcliffe decided that massive civil unrest was a good idea. It started after an unmarked police motorcycle was stolen and a day or so later it was seen being ridden by the thief. A chase ensued and the motorcycle crashed, killing the rider and pillion as they tried to evade capture.

That Thursday night certain elements of the local Hartcliffe community went on the offensive, damaging property, particularly in Symes Avenue, the shopping street for the estate. As usual, police action was blamed; it could not possibly be blamed on the social misfits, inadequates and plain criminals involved.

It was the following day, Friday, that I, as part of a police support unit, was sent into Hartcliffe from Bath (I was, by now, stationed in Bath). We were initially sent to stand by at HMS *Flying Fox*, a shore-based naval establishment, but it was only a short while later that we were dispatched to Symes Avenue to establish a line between Symes Avenue and the library. Our support unit was headed by Sergeant Jan Bebbington, a lovely lady and very good supervisor. It was quite uneventful for the first few hours; we stood there in full protective equipment consisting of flame-proof overall, flame-resistant balaclava, NATO helmet, shin guards, gloves and steel-toe-capped boots, carrying a small round shield.

How the police service had changed since 1966. But the appearance of a police officer in such equipment was not a step taken by the police by choice; it was forced on them following the St Pauls riots and other such disorder around the country.

Near to midnight we were sent to Broadbury Road Police Station to be fed, but I was so tired by then, I just could not eat. Two weeks earlier my wife, Jane, had damaged her back and had been hospitalised. For those two weeks I had been getting up early to do housework before starting duty at 7 am, then working through to 3 pm, then hospital visiting, then going home to do some more domestic chores before returning to visit again. So over two weeks my tiredness factor had gradually accumulated. At midnight on Friday I had been awake for some eighteen hours and had worked for sixteen of them.

After the break, I took over the driving seat, and surprisingly it helped wake me up. As we returned to the battleground, we drove into Bishport Avenue only seconds after all units were told not to enter the road. As we drove past the first pub, we came under a hail of bottles and stones, and then as we approached the Symes Avenue locality, I could see ahead a mass of rioters across the road – the road that we wanted to go along. I started to drive towards them and they ran at us. Again, a hail of debris. I kept moving purposefully and they fortunately moved aside. I could not help thinking about what I would have done had a couple laid down in the road. Had we stopped, we would no doubt have ended up either being dragged from the vehicle and beaten, or worse, or the personnel carrier could have been set on fire around us. The other thought was, what would have happened if I had decided that the only way I could protect the lives of myself and my six colleagues was to keep moving and run over the obstacle that blocked our way?

As we progressed into the early hours of Saturday, there were many skirmishes and pockets of violence over a widespread area of the estate. We were constantly responding to radio messages telling of officers requiring assistance. On arrival at one such call, two officers sought safety in our vehicle, one of them having been shot with an air rifle. Fortunately, the pellet had not entered his body but had caused much pain on impact.

What I can never understand is why, when dealing with riots in this country, a police shield line will chase towards the mob and cause them to scatter, then the police will stop and the mob regroups. Why do they not chase them until they reach the rioters and just beat them to the ground? After all, there are no niceties in such a situation and the police are there, despite the change of oath for those joining in 2002, to maintain the Queen's peace. The change of oath removed service to the Crown. This was done, I understand, to recruit those who were not native Brits. Well, it begs the question, why, knowing that we had a crowned head of state, did they bother to come in the first place if it presented them with a problem? I suspect it was inspired by those who are part of the so-called race-relations industry, who seek to see racism everywhere, while the majority of the ethnic minorities just carry on with life regardless and as part of the wider community. With more recent research it seems to have returned to swear to serve the king.

One of the other personnel carriers was damaged when the driver PC Tony Hunt lost control and drove into a lamp post; the control was lost when rioters entered the vehicle and tried to drag him out. Fortunately, he got away from them.

Disorder continued throughout the night, dying down only when dawn approached. I was released to return to Bath at 5 am, getting into bed at 7 am. I had been awake for twenty-six hours and working for some twenty-four of those.

I believe that during that night we, the police service, came as close as we were ever likely to losing the situation completely. The mob almost won. However, we did not retreat from the streets as we did at St Pauls.

The demands that are placed upon men and women of the police service at times are totally unrealistic. My situation during that Friday was a great example. During the morning of the Friday, I had been on patrol on my community beat. Part of the morning had been spent as the community policeman, visiting the Royal United Hospital Special School, where lovely special-needs children entertained me and their proud mums at their end-of-term play. Only some seven hours later I was supposed to be a riot policeman fending off missiles. How can a community expect men and women to change roles so drastically? What this country needs is a special riot force, trained and equipped to deal effectively with such public disorder.

Dealing with the lower end of society, the underbelly of the city, is probably the low point of most police officers' service. Sadly, the majority of people in the areas affected just want to lead their lives peacefully, but then out comes the mob. I am sure we will continue to see riots from hereon in. Until we drag society back to being disciplined, and with a sense of moral justice and responsibility, riots and massive disorder will continue. The soft liberals, who do not live in the real world, have weakened the police service so much that it is too undermined to get on top of the job.

Motorcycle Section Continued

As Traffic motorcyclists based in Bristol, much of our work was to deal with keeping the roads as free-flowing as possible so that the community could go about their business, but by the same token we also got involved in many other matters – essentially, anything that came our way: crime, summons process, etc.

In no particular order, I can recall some of them. Perhaps the lighter side to begin with.

There are those who obviously think you are stupid. I was on patrol one day, covering the wider Bath area and riding through the lovely village of Newton St Loe, when one of the villagers complained to me about the speed of a vehicle travelling along a village road. I rode along Saw Mill Lane to a dead end, where there was a small car park, and sure enough there was one vehicle with a young lady sitting in the driving seat.

'Is this your car?'

'Yes.'

I explained the nature of the complaint to her.

'I can assure you it wasn't me.'

She was the only vehicle in this cul-de-sac car park at the end of the lane.

'Did you drive here?'

'Yes.'

She then admitted that she had no documents and certainly no licence.

'But you drove it and left it here.'

'Yes.'

'How are you getting home?'

'I was going to drive.'

I then told her she was being reported for not having all necessary documents.

Forty minutes later, in Twerton Bath, I saw the same vehicle being driven by the same woman. I stopped her and said, 'I thought I told you not to drive again.'

She replied, 'Well, I couldn't get anyone to bring it back.'

Reported again for all offences.

Life must be easier nowadays, as they can seize the vehicle if not insured – good game.

Faith in Human Kind Restored

In 2006 I was baptised at Keynsham Baptist Church and became a practising Christian – however you choose to define that. I suppose I had always believed there was something else, and it was our friend June Drew who started me off on my journey into faith a few years earlier. With hindsight, and prior to June's involvement, there were two occasions where I believe God was pointing me in the direction that He eventually got me to follow.

The march to St Pauls

A number of months after the St Pauls riots, I was sent on my police motorcycle, with another motorcyclist, to St George Park to escort a march to St Pauls. There was not too much more information. We arrived there on a lovely sunny afternoon and waited.

After a short while, much to my concern we saw a very large number of young black people coming over the hill towards us. This perhaps showed the affect the riots had had on the service. However, as they reached us, a lovely young lady came up to me and explained that they were going to be marching down to St Pauls to hold a service on the green and that they had come from a national weekend convention of young black Christians at a church just up the road. Then she told me they had a band on a lorry coming, so I decided that, as I enjoyed gospel music, I should be at the front. The lorry turned up and off we set. All the way along the route, I talked to the young lady. They held their open-air service and we processed back to the church. The lorry stopped outside the church and the band continued to play. By now I had put the motorcycle on the stand, taken off my helmet and was swinging along to the music. Then the young lady came up to me and said, 'You must come to our service this evening.' Ah, what do I say to that? I explained that I could not do that because my wife was a nurse working shifts and I was babysitting. That did not deter her.

'Come tomorrow evening then.' I certainly had no excuse for Sunday and said I would try.

Sunday evening came and I put a suit on (not *a* suit, *the* suit – I only had the one) and travelled into Bristol to the church. When I entered, I immediately became an ethnic minority, one of perhaps four or five white faces. The welcome and hospitality was wonderful: lots of handshaking and waves from the band at the front. The preacher was from the West Indies and had travelled over for the weekend event and service. Well, he had passion and fire but I could hardly understand a word he said. It was a great service though, but I did nothing to follow God.

Billy Graham Crusade

In May 1984 the Billy Graham Crusade came to the Ashton Gate football stadium in Bristol. Graham was an evangelical preacher from America, who had a massive following, and this crusade was from the 12th to the 19th, with thousands attending. A team of motorcyclists, of which I was one, was given the task of escorting the buses in and crossing people over the busy A3029 Winterstoke Road. We would see them in and then later see them back across the road. As they crossed the road, they all said 'Thank you' or 'God bless you', and because of police cynicism the initial thought was that they were taking the micky, but very quickly we realised that these people were sincere in their words. What an absolute change from what we were used to.

On the final night, Billy Graham asked that we go into the ground and onto the pitch. He started the evening by thanking people for coming and then asked for thanks for those who had been marshals and there was applause. Then he thanked the first-aiders and there was applause.

Then he said, 'And last but not least, let's say thank you to the cavalry on the motorcycles who have kept us safe all week.' It was heart-stopping, the cheering and clapping that went on for some time, and I found it very emotional because all of a sudden I realised that there are thousands of people out there who actually appreciate what we do as police officers and who care about us! Even now, when I relate the story to anyone, it still brings a lump to my throat. So there was God, presumably again telling me where I should go – I should go to Him – but again I did nothing about it.

It was almost a quarter of a century later that I became a Christian follower of God. A great day.

The Lowest Point and House Arrest

On Thursday, 24 August 1989, at 2.28 pm, I attended a call to Union Street in the centre of Bristol, where a traffic warden was having problems with a driver. Upon arrival the traffic warden approached me and explained that the driver in question would not provide his name and address and he wished to report him for parking on the double yellow lines.

The defendant, a black male, then walked up to us and I explained the situation to him, telling him that he was required by law to provide his name and address. He immediately became abusive and said to the warden, 'I'm not f***ing giving my details to this f***ing disease-ridden man.' I cautioned him as to his language, as there were numerous members of the public within earshot. He continued to give a string of abuse containing the F-word.

I then decided to arrest him for offensive conduct and I radioed for assistance. And as I did so, he walked back to the car. I approached him and stood by him to prevent him from moving away. He moved to one side and I took hold of his arm and told him I was arresting him for offensive conduct. He then pushed against me and I pushed him back against his car and restrained him. A struggle ensued and I felt the driver's knee make contact with my groin. I continued to restrain him and was shortly joined by a patrol-car crew. Together with one of the officers, and against significant resistance, I handcuffed him, but only after having to hold him firmly over his car bonnet, during which time his spectacles were dislodged. I picked them up carefully and handed them to the other car-crew member. Eventually, after a struggle, he was put into the patrol car and conveyed to the Central Police Station. There, during a search of the prisoner, a brown paper wrap containing vegetable matter was found in his pocket.

At 3.50 pm I took a statement from the warden and then wrote up my own statement at 4.30 pm. The defendant was known to the police and also used an alias.

At 5.10 pm I was informed that a certain senior officer in the Complaints and Discipline Department wanted to speak to me and that I was not to leave the station.

At 5.20 pm I was seen by the senior officer who told me not to leave the station. I furnished him with a photocopy of my statement and a photocopy of my pocket notebook entries. He left.

At 6.20 pm the acting duty inspector at the station told me that the aforementioned senior officer would be back in ten minutes to see me again.

At 6.32 pm he came to see me and told me I could not return to my Traffic station 'for obvious reasons'. He asked me what I wanted to do. I told him I wanted to return to my station to have my refreshments and a game of snooker. I then added, 'Or go out and do the job I'm paid to do.'

He immediately replied, 'Well, *I'm* doing the job *I'm* paid to do. This man is politically sensitive and it will be all over the papers tomorrow, so we have to do it right.'

I objected to being placed under virtual house arrest. He asked me if I wished to see a doctor. I said I would submit an Injury on Duty Form when I returned to my station and then, if necessary, see my own doctor in the morning (this was relating to the attempted knee in my genitals). He replied that it would be better to see the police doctor and he would arrange it.

By now I was increasingly concerned that I was being fitted up for having unlawfully arrested a black man, a so-called community leader. As a result, I kept my pocket notebook up to date, and after every entry I made a fresh photocopy, secreting it on my person.

At 7.25 pm I was sent to the Photographic Department, where a somewhat embarrassed police photographer told me he had to take photos of my genitals. I pointed out that there was no sign of injury but that he should do what he had to.

At approximately 7.40 pm I was seen by the police doctor, who spent time on a cursory examination of the top half of my body, then a similar cursory examination of the lower half of my body, but did not actually examine my genitals!

At 7.50 pm I was told by the senior officer to go home – I was not due to finish until 10 pm. I asked if I could go back to my station and do report writing, as I did not want to get home early and worry my wife, who was due to go into hospital for an operation very soon. This had no effect on him at all, and I was again told to go home. I went back to my station, where my motorcycle sergeant took me into an office to ask me what was happening, and the whole sorry episode and the accompanying stress caused me to break down in tears. The stress and concern I experienced as a result of doing my job completely lawfully just chopped me off at the knees.

At 8.45 pm, having recovered my composure, I got on my personal motorcycle and rode to Keynsham Police Station, where I stayed drinking tea until about 10.15 pm, at which point I rode home, arriving at my normal time.

The following morning I was in work at 10 am and had a meeting with my inspector, Ted Allen, a perfect gentleman. I then went to the Police Federation office before going to see my chief superintendent and another superintendent. Then I went back to the Federation office to apply for legal advice because I remained in a state of real fear that I was to be fitted up, all because my prisoner was a so-called politically sensitive black man.

At 2.04 pm I was back at Avon Street Traffic Centre, where I was again seen by the original senior officer from Complaints and Discipline, who served me a Regulation 7 notice – unbelievable – for doing my duty. He cautioned me and asked me if I had anything to say, and my reply was, 'If I did not have a mortgage, I would be telling you to stick your job!' Even now I am surprised I gave that response! Indicative of the continuing stress.

After a number of months, I was contacted by the senior officer, who told me that no further action was being taken – action on what? I ask myself – and then asked me if I wanted the photographs that had been taken! I told him I did not see any reason for them in the first place, so why would I want them now.

After thirty-one years' service, I cannot think of any police officer I despise, other than this little senior officer, a very nasty little man. Do I bear a grudge? Yes, you bet I do!

Bath

In September 1997 I started a three-month temporary transfer to Bath. This came about in a strange way. There was, and perhaps still is, something called an Informal Resolution within the discipline code. If someone complains about you, then, with your agreement, it can be informally resolved, as long as the complainant is also happy, as I recall.

It was either late 1996 or early 1997 when I had a very positive staff appraisal with my chief inspector, all very complimentary. A short while later I was told by him that I was being moved off Traffic, as I had received a total of nine Informal Resolution complaints over, as I recall, a twelve-month period. The official line was that they did not tally up Informal Resolutions. If you say so! This 'punishment' came as a massive shock to me, to the extent that on the day I was told, my chief inspector said he would drive me home, as he could clearly see what a significant and profound shock it was. When I returned to work, they asked me where I wished to be transferred to and I chose the city of Bath. I had no wish to continue working in the city of Bristol. However, I felt that I was subject to an injustice. I decided to wade through my pocket notebooks for the twelve months in question and found that during that period I had dealt with over 900 offenders – either by arrest, endorsable fixed penalties, non-endorsable fixed penalties or verbal cautions – so just 1 per cent of the people I had dealt with over the period had complained. I then put together a report seeking an interview with the deputy chief constable, the late John Harland. I presented my case to him and informed him about the staff appraisal, which he did not have in his possession. He said, 'So you are saying there is much more good about you than bad?"

'Yes, sir,' I replied.

He then said he would look into it.

It was some weeks later that I was summoned to his office. He said, 'I have decided that you will stay on Traffic in Bristol, but had your chief superintendent counselled you on this, it might be a different matter.'

I thanked him and went back to my motorcycle duties. However, it was to my surprise how much of a mental toll this took on me. The anxiety was enormous, constantly wondering what would happen if just one member of the public complained that, in dealing with his breach of the law, he was not best pleased with me. Would that mean I was for immediate transfer? Every day I climbed into my leathers I could feel my stomach tightening up. In an effort to try to overcome this, Jane and I went away for a break in mid Wales. We stayed in a log cabin on a holiday site. It was just three or four nights but quite relaxing. It came to our last day, so we loaded up the car and drove down to the main road, turning left towards home. Immediately upon heading home, I felt my stomach tightening up. This was ridiculous and not at all like me. It did not take much to convince myself that I just could not carry on like this and that I needed to leave the motorcycle section and Traffic, where I had worked hard and dedicated twenty years of my service.

I sat down and wrote a report asking for a temporary transfer to the city of Bath. It was not long in coming, and I dusted off my foot patrol helmet and arrived in Bath in September 1990. Upon arrival I was told that for the first week I would have the 'Bath experience', or in other words, walking a beat in the city centre. What an 'experience' it was, indeed. It really was so good being back on foot, interacting with members of the public in a positive and helpful way rather than being in a confrontational situation, reporting them for a traffic offence or worse.

That said, I did have a couple of arrests in the first week or two. Things had changed along the way since I was last on foot patrol, because there were looks of absolute surprise from another officer when I turned down the offer of a lift in a police car with my prisoner, choosing instead to walk him, perhaps half a mile, from the city centre to the police station, with his arm up his back! Probably, today that might be breaching his human rights! A different world. Not necessarily a better one.

Something I found amusing during that first week was being a tourist attraction. Bath is one of only two complete cities to be a World Heritage Site; the other is Venice. In September half of America and the world and its brother are in the city. I recall being stopped at the bottom of Stall Street, near Marks & Spencer, when an American approached me and asked whether he could take a photograph. 'Yes, of course' was the answer. 'Oh! With your wife and her mother? Okay.' As they moved away, a queue of people wanting to take my photograph had formed. All foreigners, of course. It took me the best part of twenty minutes to walk to the top of Milsom Street, a journey which might normally take six or seven minutes.

On the topic of tourists, I well recall meeting two female teachers from Germany in Gay Street. Talking to them, I discovered this was their first trip abroad, despite being in their thirties (or thereabouts), as they had lived in East Germany. It was just short of a year after the Berlin Wall was torn down on 9 November 1989. They just oozed freedom.

Life was just great from my perspective; I really should have done this years before!

It was probably only day three or four of the first week when I decided that there was absolutely nothing to go back to the Traffic Department for, and within a month I had asked that my transfer be made permanent.

I was then given a community beat covering Twerton, on the western extremes of the city, an area with a bit of a reputation. However, once there, it was clear it was not as bad as had been suggested. On one of my first days on the patch I decided I would check the licensed premises; in other words, a uniformed visit to the pubs to ensure they were being run correctly. At the first one I entered, in Twerton High Street, mine host's first question was, 'So where are you going to be drinking?' He seemed quite surprised when I told him, 'Nowhere while on duty'. Apparently, there might have been a different practice before me!

As the new boy on the city policing, I was still getting used to different police officers. One evening, I was on my patch when a police car came up with the blue light going. It slowed to a stop and explained that there had been a stabbing at some flats, so I said I would go with them, as it was on my patch. In the car were two mature policemen. We got to the flat, and a woman had stabbed a man, not fatally. Steve, one of the guys dealing with her, came across to me after a while and said, 'I need to arrest her but she tells me there is no one to look after the kids. What should I do?' Now, Steve was in his late thirties, I believe, and I found it most amusing that here was *he* asking *me* what to do, when I had been a Traffic officer for the last twenty years. What I did not know was that

Steve was in fact a late-starting, mature recruit with just a few months' service.

So what was the answer to his question? Well, very simple really. I went to the woman and told her that my colleague needed to arrest her, and again she trotted out the fact that there was no one to have the kids. 'No problem,' I said. 'It will only take a very short time to get social services here and we can soon have them in care, so you do not have to worry about them.' It was amazing how quickly she was able to ask a neighbour to babysit. Steve was impressed and learnt a lesson, I am sure, that flannel works wonders at times!

There was a second occasion, when, in a hurry, I visited a flat in Twerton. It was sometime after I had left that beat for a new one, but I was, as I recall, covering a night or late shift until 2 am. I was with another community beat officer, Paul, at Bath Police Station when the call came in that a father had come home drunk, had grabbed the baby and had a knife. The caller was the mother of the baby. We leapt into the car and set off at speed. It did not take us too long to reach the building. On arrival the mum was at the door in a very distressed state. She had the front door open at the bottom of a flight of stairs that led to the first-floor flat. So we were there for a reason – man armed with knife holding baby – and we were the police, so in and up we went. I was ahead of Paul, and as we approached the landing there was Dad with the baby in his hands. Fortunately, the knife in question was sticking out of the back pocket of his trousers, so I quickly grabbed Dad and pushed him back against a wall on the landing, while Paul grabbed the knife from Dad's back pocket. Dad was clearly under the influence of alcohol. Many times I asked him to let the baby go. The baby by now was very distressed, as indeed was Mum, who had followed us up and was standing in the doorway of the lounge, off the landing. I was concerned that the baby might be harmed by the father. I asked again, and there was no reasoning with him. I decided that in the interest of the baby's welfare I had to take proportionate action. The only answer was to hit him, and as he was holding the baby, the only exposed part of his body was his head. I punched him as hard as I could in the eye and then without delay delivered a second punch. As it landed, he let go of the baby. Gravity took a hand and the baby headed for the floor. Fortunately, I managed to catch it by the head, which was not good, but I managed to bend at the knees so that its little body stopped on my thighs. The baby was passed to Mum, and Dad was arrested.

Early the following morning I was telephoned at home by Tim, a detective constable. 'Remind me never to pick a fight with you' was his opening statement. He asked whether I had seen the state of my prisoner, telling me that his face was swollen and one eye was closed and bruised. He told me that my prisoner, the dad, was in a cell next to a very noisy prisoner who had kept him awake shouting that he wanted to make a complaint against the police. When Tim went to Dad's cell, Dad asked if he could speak to the man next door. Tim took him to the hatch, whereupon Dad shouted at him to shut up and told him, 'Look. This is what they did to me. I deserved it and I'm making no complaint, so be quiet.' When he was interviewed he made no complaint, accepted that everything he did was wrong, particularly involving the baby, and said, 'When he punched me, I was going to give the baby up, but before I could he punched me again!'

You, the police, have to win. A different world then. Arguably, a better world.

Newbridge and Lower Weston Community Beat

My darling wife, Jane, was at this time a nurse on the Accident & Emergency Department of the Royal United Hospital, and the hospital stood within the Newbridge and Lower Weston community beat area, so a great attraction to seek to be the community policeman. It seems that I had a supporter in Chief Inspector Jenny Walton because she supported my application and then it was mine. Jenny Walton was an old-style police officer and very much a leader. I remember once at a Bristol Rovers football match – well, it was the aftermath of the match – there was large-scale disorder in the street and Jenny was there at the front of her officers, leading, not following. I had, and have, great respect for the lady – probably, the best chief inspector I have served under. If she had reason to speak to you about anything you had done wrong, once spoken the matter was forgotten and life continued as normal.

This was to be the start of seven wonderful years, taking me through to my retirement from the police. I viewed it as a super new chapter, not a back water to slow down for retirement.

The community beat was quite varied and part of it covered the world-famous Royal Crescent and Royal Victoria Park, including the Botanical Gardens, a whole range of housing stock – big private houses through to, for the most part, tidy council housing – and the jewel in the crown, the Royal United Hospital and the acute psychiatric hospital, Hillview Lodge. Nearby there were also community psychiatric houses.

Though I was within seven years of retirement, I did not see this as an easy number. At the time, I described the role as three different professions; I had to be a demolition expert to break down barriers, a builder to build bridges and a salesman to promote and sell the worth of the police service to the public. In those tasks I believe I succeeded.

Becoming the policeman responsible for the Royal United Hospital was amazing, and soon after starting I decided to establish a Hospital Watch to encourage staff and visitors alike to be vigilant in spotting potential crime or people acting suspiciously. To support this, I convinced the service that it would be good to make a video to promote it. This was agreed, then I needed an on-screen presenter, and I had no doubt who I would use: someone in a nursing uniform, someone well spoken and someone reliable. No contest then! Mrs Hale took a little bit of convincing but eventually agreed. I used the video on every talk I gave to staff and incoming staff members.

I built good relationships with the security team at the hospital. They were all very keen guys trying to do their best and were very appreciative of the support and backing I gave them.

Hospital theft

Sadly, there was a great deal of crime on-site; clearly, the criminal classes saw it as a soft touch, but sadly so did the occasional staff member. What I found unfortunate was that when there was a theft, there was too often the assumption by medical staff that it must have been the cleaners. On one occasion it was certainly a porter.

The staff from the hospital shop found that on a Sunday it was always missing a paper when they collected the bundle of newspapers from near the porter's lodge, so one Sunday, early, as the papers were dropped, I arranged to have the top paper marked. Sure enough, the shop staff collected and one paper was missing. So along to the lodge I went and found the supervising porter sat comfortably reading the paper. He admitted the theft of the paper and was arrested. Petty, you might think. That is, until we took him to search his house, where there was a whole catalogue of hospital property: sheets, pillowcases, mattress covers, blankets, fifteen NHS dinner plates, an extension lead, tea towels, plus a shopping list of hospital catering supplies.

For the sake of saving a pound or two on a Sunday newspaper, this widespread theft from his employers left him without a job, and rightly so.

Body friendly

Despite having served on the Roads Policing Unit for twenty years, I only dealt with one fatal collision, and on that occasion, someone else accompanied the body to the mortuary. In fact, I had little to do with bodies, even back on my Territorial Division days, and was put off during my probation when we had to go and watch a post-mortem. An acquired taste that some acquire and others do not.

However, here I was with a major general hospital on my beat and with an Accident & Emergency Department, where casualties often die a sudden death. This is a death where the doctors cannot identify the cause of the death and thus the body has to be subjected to a post-mortem. At the point of dying a sudden death, the body becomes the property of Her Majesty's Coroner for the district. He or she, of course, does not attend the scene of death. There is a local coroner's officer, often a retired police officer, but they also rarely attend the scene of death, and so the task is rolled down the hill until it reaches the police constable on the ground. In my case, as the PC covering the hospital, I had a fair supply of deaths.

Very quickly I found myself becoming more body-friendly. Because of the number of deaths – and therefore the number of relatives of the deceased – I was dealing with, I decided I had to do something to make me more able. I signed up for a course called Understanding Bereavement run by the bereavement counselling service Cruse Bereavement Care. At the end of the course there was an opportunity to move on to complete a bereavement counselling course, so that is what I did, and once qualified I did some bereavement counselling.

The course made me feel more empowered when dealing with grieving relatives. You need to understand that these relatives are at their lowest ebb, having just lost a loved one. If the police make a hash of dealing with them, they will be considered a load of buffoons for the rest of that person's life. However, if they are supported and handled in a professional and empathetic manner, the police will be looked upon positively in the future; it might even cancel out any future negative encounters they might have. I know I got it right because I have letters and cards from relatives that support that fact.

Before I retired I was told that statistically a police officer deals with, on average, one and a half sudden deaths per year. In my last two years of service I dealt with thirty-three such deaths. While they all involved a body, they were all different in need and detail.

One that I attended at the hospital A & E Department stands out in my memory. Aaban (not his real name) was but a small baby still in a Moses basket and had been brought in dead by the father and two adult male relatives. They were a Muslim family from Wiltshire. I suppose my first surprise was that Mum was not present, but it was not for me to question that. I did all the necessary paperwork and then it was explained to me that the burial had to take place within twenty-four hours; cremation is strictly forbidden within the Muslim faith.

I now had the challenge of finding a funeral director who was able to accomplish such a funeral, as well as the job of finding a suitable burial ground. All of this activity took place in the relative's room at A & E, with little Aaban lying peacefully in his Moses basket on the floor. These challenges were overcome, but there was one other obstacle.

Paediatric sudden deaths were also subject to post-mortem. At the RUH the body had to be conveyed to the Bristol Children's Hospital for the post-mortem and I had to explain this to the father and the relatives. That fact was accepted, but then he asked whether they could collect Aaban from the Children's Hospital rather than the undertaker collecting him. I asked why and they explained that the body needed to be washed and prepared as required in the Muslim faith. I then had to ask whether they knew what a post-mortem was. The answer was that they were not sure. I described it as being something like an operation but the stitching was not the neat job you might expect after an operation. They accepted my explanation and hopefully this prepared them for the appearance of little Aaban once he returned home.

Another cot death also in my memory is that of an even younger child. Again, in such circumstances it is necessary to inspect the body, as one does with an adult death, and this means getting down to skin level. So it was with this little child. All seemed okay until we reached the rectal area, where we found traces of a gel or lubricant. Suddenly, there were doctors most concerned that the child had been abused sexually. Thankfully, before too many hares started running, a nurse mentioned that when the child had been brought in, they had taken the temperature of the body with a rectal thermometer aided by a lubricant!

One morning the body of a young man was found hanged on my patch and was thus conveyed to the hospital, where was pronounced dead on arrival. His parents were called and by the time they arrived – they had a little way to come – the body had been moved to the mortuary and placed in the viewing room, with the usual garment that covered the body up to the chin. I accompanied the mum and her partner to the mortuary and initially went into the viewing room, receiving confirmation from her that this was in fact her son. Having established this, as was my normal practice I asked whether she would like some time alone with him, and she said yes. I withdrew to the waiting room, which was adjacent. After a short while she came out and said in quite a matter-of-fact way, 'Can I come back to see him tomorrow when the rope has been removed?' It had not entered my head that she might find the rope, which had been left in situ for the post-mortem. Clearly and understandably, she had held him or cuddled him when I had left.

Perhaps the most difficult and emotional sudden death I

handled was again at the RUH. On the previous evening a young woman, a university student, was making her way home when she stopped outside one of the Georgian terraces and leant on the metal fence, only to find that the bit she had leant on was in fact the gate to the basement flat. She fell into the basement courtyard and suffered catastrophic head injuries. I was called to the hospital on the Sunday, as her parents had arrived, having had to travel from some distance away. Sadly, their task was to give permission to turn off the life-support machine, as there was no way back for their daughter. I decided that the pragmatic way of dealing with the situation was to take all the details necessary to complete my Sudden Death Form while the daughter was still 'alive'. The parents agreed to this; it meant that once their daughter had 'died', with the removal of the life support, I would not need to complete a form and they could grieve in peace. The emotional challenge for me was that the predominant age profile of sudden deaths was late middle age to old age, whereas here I was dealing with the death of a young woman about the same age as my eldest daughter. That was heart-wrenching.

Perhaps the oddest sudden death was more a death message rather than the actual sudden-death process. A motorcyclist had been killed in a collision on a five-ways nasty junction outside of Bath, just in Wiltshire, and his body had been conveyed to a hospital some distance outside of Bath, in Swindon. I was asked to deliver the news to the widow. It was a lovely sunny day and when I arrived outside the house a young woman was in the front garden tending the plants. I approached her and she identified herself as the person I was looking for. I asked if we could go into the house, which we did. Once in I told her the bad news, which she took very calmly. She then said to me, 'You know he left me six weeks ago?' Ah! Not the response I was expecting. I asked if there was anything I could do for her, and despite the calm, and the desertion of her late husband, she still wanted to view him. So I told her I would drive her to Swindon, but we collected her in-laws on the way because they were still on good terms with her. We conducted the identification and I gained some more details. We were still at the hospital when I got a call from my sergeant saying that she was with the deceased's new partner and she too wanted to view the body. Ah! I had to convince my sergeant to delay that for an hour or so but also told her that if the partner wanted to ring me at home that evening, I would talk her through everything. This was agreed. So a potentially very awkward meeting was avoided. That evening I talked with the partner, a nurse, for almost an hour – counselling again.

Death messages: how to deliver?

Giving the death message is not an exact science but is a task that many officers would prefer not to deal with. Becoming more confident in the task really came during my time as a community beat officer and also following my Cruse Understanding Bereavement course, because back then, and perhaps even now, death and bereavement were not things that were taught.

The easiest way might be viewed as the starker way. Compassion is obviously the underlying approach, but once you have established that the person in front of you is indeed the next of kin, the only thing to say is, 'I am very sorry but your husband (or daughter, father, etc.) has been killed in a car crash (or whatever fate has befallen him or her).'

The important word in this very short statement is 'killed', or it could be 'died', but it only causes confusion if euphemisms are used:

'I am afraid your husband will not be coming home!'
'Why? Where is he? Is he working late?'
'I am sorry but your wife has passed!'
'Passed where? I hope she will be back soon; I have to go to work!'

You understand the picture?

Bereavement takes many forms, but it is suggested that there are varying stages. Five could be classed as: denial, anger, bargaining, depression and acceptance.

The NHS offers different headings: accepting that the loss is real, experiencing the pain of grief, adjusting to life without that person, putting less emotional energy into grieving and more into something new. (This one seems a bit dismissive to me. Okay, he's dead. Stop fretting. Why don't you join the Women's Institute?)

So not an exact science, but one reaction that the officer might experience upon delivering the death message is anger, expressed either through emotions or even physical actions. It is at this time that compassion and understanding has to play a very big part. Equally, the anger might be expressed towards the deceased: 'I told him not to buy that bloody motorbike' or 'He did not need to go into work today, but would he listen? Would he hell!'

The question of identifying the deceased is important because we need to be sure that the body in the mortuary is the person we believe them to be. The process is not just to identify though; it is part of the grieving process because there may well be denial that this is not real, and viewing the loved one's dead body makes it real, painful as it might be. My own view is that children should also take the opportunity to view the body – perhaps not the very young but certainly those in their teens – if not in the mortuary's chapel of rest then certainly at the funeral company's chapel of rest. I never viewed my dad after his death and I regret it now, the chance to say that last farewell.

I was amazed at my two granddaughters when my step-mum-in-law died in the nursing home. Almost the whole family had gathered around the bed, including the two girls, who were perhaps 14 and 15. They were present as June drew her last breath and then remained sitting at her side for some time, certainly an hour or so.

Perhaps it happens elsewhere, but of all the hospital-based sudden deaths I dealt with identification either took place in a cubicle at A & E immediately after the death or, if there was a time delay waiting for relatives, in a tasteful chapel of rest at the mortuary. I always find it most alien when TV and films portray identification taking place on a post-mortem slab or by pulling a metal body-bearing tray from the fridge. I would hope that such identification does not happen this way in real life.

My advice to the relatives after the formal work was over was that there is no formal or prescribed way of grieving; whichever way they grieve is the right way. No one gives you a checklist. I also advised them not to be pushed down roads other people believed they should take as far as the funeral was concerned. I would tell them that whatever they or the deceased had wanted should be the way to do it.

One of the benefits of my Cruse bereavement training was that I was able to organise a few training sessions at Bath Police Station for my colleagues, and I was supported in delivering them by Rev Chris Roberts, the hospital chaplain, and Senior Charge Nurse Pete Fox from the A & E Department at the Royal United Hospital. We also did one for the nursing staff, who do not always receive bereavement training.

It was always very moving to receive letters and cards of thanks for doing my job when dealing with sudden deaths, but it clearly indicated that doing the job properly can have an immense effect on the lives of those left behind.

I was amazed when in 2003, after retirement and upon being made senior road safety officer for South Gloucestershire Council (it being reported in the press), I received a congratulations card from a lady, together with a letter reminding me that thirteen years earlier I had dealt with the death of her mother in a road collision and telling me how much the assistance I had given her was appreciated.

Alan Hale Esq
Senior Road Safety Officer
South Gloucestershire Council
Broad Lane
Engine Common Lane
YATE
South Glos
BS37 7PN   21 August 2003

Dear Alan,

Having seen your picture in the Evening Post, I had to write to congratulate you on your new appointment.

I have not forgotten the support you gave me on the death of my mother – Gladys Rees - following a road traffic accident on the crossing in Brislington village. This was a long time ago – April 1990 – but your assistance was very much appreciated. I am sure you will be a great success in your new position.

Thank you once again.

Kindest regards

Gerry

Death, of course, is very distressing whichever form it takes. It does not have to be a human death. We have had four dogs since we married. There was Mick, a corgi we inherited upon the divorce of Jane's parents; Mick eventually had to be put down. Then a while later, along came Cindy, a cross-breed, but we were never sure between what; a nice dog with, at times, a temperamental streak. Sadly, in later life Cindy suffered heart problems and she too had to be put down. Then, when we were 'never going to have another dog', we got Sam, a cross between a Border terrier and a Lakeland terrier. Jane had wanted a bitch, and having driven some distance to the breeders on the far side of Bath and then finding that what was on offer was a male pup, Jane said no. We drove all the way back home and as we stopped outside our house, Jane remarked that had it been a baby we would not have known the sex. I restarted the engine and off we went on the journey back to the breeder. Sam was a lovely dog with a great temperament, but sadly, as the years passed, he contracted cancer and also had to be relieved of his suffering. Now, in 2022, we have Lexi, a Jackapoo, again an amazing temperament and lovely character. Again, a dog that we were never going to have after Sam!

My Chief Constable's Commendation

On Thursday, 10 January 1991, just after midday, I was in the Peugeot car dealership on Upper Bristol Road chatting to one of the salesmen when I heard a call on my radio that a young man had been seen loading a handgun at Royal Victoria Park. The park was directly opposite, but the report was from the top end and it said the man had gone into the Botanical Gardens.

To get there was uphill and I had no intention of running that far and uphill! (As if I could achieve it anyway!) I came out onto the road and immediately commandeered a driver and his car to take me to the top of Park Lane, where I went into the park and was shortly joined by a Traffic officer.

As I looked into the gardens, I saw the young man in question. It was definitely him, as he had been reported as wearing a Davey Crockett type of hat, and there was the hat on his head. I asked the Traffic man to give me a leg up to get over the high metal fence. As I dropped to the ground, the young man came out from behind a tree some 20 metres away. He had a bag in one hand and his other hand was in his pocket. Was this the hand with the gun? I started to walk towards him and called to him. He started to walk towards me.

In these circumstances, what else would you do other than keep moving towards him? After all, I was the one in the police uniform, and part of the deal is that you do not step back! After a very short moment, I was close to him – close enough to grab the arm of the hand that was in his pocket and throw him to the ground. Having restrained him, I was able to look in the bag, and there I found a loaded air pistol – the type of pistol that might encourage you to put your hands up if asked nicely!

Other officers had arrived, including Inspector Ian Lock, a lovely man who passed away many years too soon after retirement. As we came out of the gardens, Ian said that once the case file had been put together he wanted a copy. This, he told me, was to recommend me for a Chief Constable's Commendation. This he did, and some while later a ceremony was held at Bath Police Station, where Chief Constable David Shattock presented me with the Certificate of Commendation. David was a policeman's policeman and a great chief constable.

Knives

As I continue to write this in 2022, knife crime is prevalent and high on the agenda. Much of it is black on black but you clearly never know when or from where the threat will come. Thankfully, I had only four occasions where knives were a potential threat. All four were on extended late shifts or nights and three of the four were once I had transferred to Bath. These occurred many years before stab vests or body armour.

In April 1988, late one afternoon, I responded to a call to the Playhouse Launderette on Gloucester Road, Bristol, where it was reported that a man was brandishing a knife. Upon my arrival PC Tony Court and a policewoman, PC Streete, were already there. PC Court had taken possession of a knife and sheath. He was talking to the offender. Suddenly, the offender made a grab for the sheath knife, but PC Court was quick enough to twist it from the offender's grip. PC Court then moved forward to arrest the offender and took hold of his left arm. The offender immediately swung his right arm and punched PC Court in the face and then wrapped his arm around his neck in a neck lock. My recollection is that I had already taken my handcuffs from my belt. Together with PC Streete, I tried to pull the offender off PC Court. The offender continued to struggle violently and was obviously a very powerful man, as he continued to hold PC Court in a neck lock. I was by now concerned as to our ability to successfully restrain and arrest him, so my next move was to punch him as hard as I could in the face – a proportionate response, in my opinion He fell to the ground and I handcuffed him. He was conveyed to Redland Police Station, still struggling violently, and once we had him in the charge office, I realised that he had a significant cut to his face. I can only assume that when I punched him, I did so with the hand holding the handcuffs! The custody sergeant looked at his wound and asked, 'Who did this?'

I replied, 'I believe I did, during the arrest.'

Truth is always a good answer and nothing more was said of the injury. Another bad man off of the streets for a while.

The problem is that when the calls are received and a knife is mentioned, you attend knowing there is a risk, but not necessarily to you personally. One such call was to a flat on Upper Bristol Road in Bath, and upon entering, there was a man sitting on a settee with a knife in his hand but making threats to stab himself, so that lowered the risk initially – well, for me! However, I could not stand and watch a self-stabbing, so I began to talk to the man, but he was very difficult to engage with. This went on for some time, with him pushing the knife against his abdomen every so often. I had already drawn my extendable baton for self-protection if needed. A while later the duty sergeant came into the flat, and at one point the man appeared distracted, so I took the chance to strike him on the legs and then grab his arms to prevent him making a potentially fatal stabbing, either to himself or to me. Job done.

On Sunday, 17 November 1996, having just dealt with a sudden death at the A & E Department of the Royal United Hospital, Bath, I was called to one of the medical wards, and once there I spoke to a staff nurse who told me that on two occasions she had heard a patient voice threats to kill his parents. I went to speak to him. After a number of attempts to engage with him, he rolled over to speak with me, but upon seeing that I was a police officer he said, 'I knew they would do that.'

I naturally assumed he meant the staff. I said, 'Why is that?'

'Because I said I was going to kill my parents!'

I said, 'You don't really mean that, do you?'

'Just watch me!'

'I am arresting you for making threats to kill,' I cautioned him. I told him to get up and he rolled over and produced an open knife. Thankfully, he was holding the blade.

He said, 'I suppose you will want this.' I took it from him and he then said, 'I'll kill them anyway.'

The lesson from that simple call was that in the controlled environment of a hospital ward a knife could easily have been used to stab and perhaps kill a member of the medical staff or me, or indeed one or more patients!

On 22 December, just one month later, I again responded to a call of a violent domestic where a knife was involved. This was again in Bath at a house in Broadway. Upon arrival I was soon joined by a couple of other officers. The report of the presence of a knife was repeated by the informant and one other member of the public.

I equipped myself with a short shield and drew my ASP. (The ASP was the new metal version of the wooden truncheon and collapsed within itself to about six to eight inches in length. To 'rack' it or open it you swung it forcibly and the collapsed sections flew out and locked in place.) I went to the front door of the house. We were heading for the flat on the first floor; I was in front and some officers were behind me. Another officer rang the intercom bell and the door was unlocked. I then led us up the stairs to the front door of the flat, and upon knocking it was opened by a woman who we later found to be the tenant. She was in an extremely distressed condition, and standing immediately behind her was a man whose hands I could not see.

She said, 'Everything's all right now', a typical domestic situation and response.

I said, 'Well, we want to make sure", and I moved forward. She did not object and walked back into the flat from the confined hallway. This gave me a clear view of the male. While at that point he had nothing in his hands, I could not be sure he was not armed. I asked him to move into the room but he stood still and started to argue. I racked my ASP and shouted the instruction to move back into the room. He walked into the room and I shouted at him to get down on the floor face down. Again he argued and again I shouted the instruction to get down on the floor. This time he dropped to the floor and extended his arms sideways when told. I then stepped beyond him, and another PC searched him for weapons but found nothing. He was told he could get up just some thirty seconds later. He declined and said he would stay there.

My final act was to check the kitchen, always the most dangerous room in the house – so many potential weapons. I then left the others to deal with the domestic issues. Again a call that had the potential to go wrong, with the possibility of people being injured, or worse. My only closing thought as I left was why, at 49 years of age and the oldest officer in attendance, I had ended up being the first through the door. The answer, of course, was simple: whatever my age, I was still an active and keen police officer, so it was part of the job – an exciting part of the job!

One evening in June 1997, at 7.05 pm, I attended a house in Hampton View, Bath, where a disturbance had been reported. Upon arrival I found the front door with a smashed pane of glass, and standing inside the door, which was closed, was the occupier covered in blood, shouting and acting in an agitated way, clearly not in his right mind.

Not a problem, until his very aged and deaf mother wandered into view and stood by him. Reasoning did not achieve anything, so I moved nearer, but he then started spitting blood at me and the others through the broken pane. After some while, getting nowhere with talking, I decided that the only way forward was to gas him. Out came the canister. I gave it a good shake and then told him what was going to happen if he did not calm down and open the door. My main fear was for his mother and what he might do to her. Still no compliance. I then tried to get his mother to move away from him, and that was a challenge, as I do not think she comprehended what I was saying. Then at one moment she moved away and I immediately sprayed him with the incapacitant. Sadly, his mother then decided to walk back next to him and also received some of the cloud, but it did not seem to cause her problems. I was then able to put my hand through the broken window to release the door and gain entry to drag him out. Unfortunately, as we did this his mother walked back through the gas cloud into a back room. We could not leave her in the house in case the spray had a detrimental effect on her, so, as it was my spray and I was first there, I decided I would have to go in and retrieve her. If I did this, I would of course receive a small dose of my own medicine as I passed through the remains of the gas cloud and then re-passed as I brought his mother out. Still, though, the spray seemed not to have had any effect on her. She was cared for by a neighbour while we took her son to the police station. I followed as a passenger in another car, with my head hanging out of the window for the duration of the journey, trying to clear my eyes of the spray. Job done.

Psychiatric patients played a big part in my role as a community policeman, as within the grounds of the Royal United Hospital was Hillview Lodge, the main chronic psychiatric hospital for the Bath and Wiltshire Health Trust, and there were also three residential homes nearby.

When I arrived on my beat I decided it would be important to visit these facilities, as I believed it was likely, due to their illnesses, that the patients might well come into contact with the police, and my thinking was that if I could break down barriers the uniform might create, it would help the patients and also any future police officers.

It has to be said that my fellow officers were never keen to deal with anything at Hillview, often offering the excuse that they could not always tell who were the staff (they did not wear uniform) and who were the patients. I always used to say that if you talked to everyone the same as you would normally, you would eventually reveal those who were ill.

One of my early encounters came on a late turn one evening,

crewed with a policewoman. A certain patient, who I shall only call Barry (not his real name), was reported as having absconded from the unit. Over the radio came the warning that he would probably need four officers to detain him and get him back. As I drove down Combe Park, there at the bottom of the road, going into a pub, was Barry, or so the description suggested. Barry was a 6-foot-plus, well-built black man carrying a guitar. Anyway, we were there now, so we parked the car and went into the pub and found Barry at the bar with a pint in front of him.

'Hello, Barry,' I said. 'We have to take you back to the hospital.'

There was no immediate response, so I became a tad concerned.

'I have only just got my pint,' said Barry slowly.

'No problem. There is no rush. Finish your pint then we will give you a lift back up to the hospital.'

He finished his pint and walked out to the car with us and we had no problem at all returning him. It might well have needed four officers if I had not used my ability to talk to people. The mouth is the policeman's best tool.

After that, when we met up either out on the street, when he was not sectioned, or in the unit, when he was sectioned under the Mental Health Act, he would always chat to me very respectfully and ask after another colleague, Colin Britton, who had also probably treated him with respect and care. On only one occasion did I have some concern with Barry. It was an afternoon and he had again absconded and was believed to be heading for home. I said I would go to his home and bring him back. He let me into his flat, where he showed me some of his outstanding artwork and carried on as though I was just a visitor. I then explained that I had come to pick him up to take him back to Hillview. Nothing much changed and it probably took twenty minutes of talking to get him out through the door. There was no point trying to use force, as he would have won. As we got into the car, he continuously stared at me, which gave me a little cause for concern. I told him to put his seat belt on but I deliberately did not put mine on, so on the drive back I kept the speed low just in case it all blew up and I had to make a quick exit from the car! Thankfully, despite the staring, the journey was successfully accomplished.

While not connected to Hillview, one late evening I found a wanted man walking through the hospital grounds. We will call him Mike Stone. He was quite a stocky, powerful-looking man. I walked over to him and told him I needed to talk with him about a warrant that had been issued for his arrest. He responded by saying, 'Just leave me alone, Mr Hale. I want to go home.' I told him I could not do that, and as he was clearly not going to comply, I drew and racked my ASP, moved in front of him and told him to stop. He stood still and asked whether I was going to hit him with it. In a loud, and hopefully threatening, voice I told him I would and to get down on the ground. He immediately sat down and waited quietly for the car to arrive to convey him to the police station. Probably a few months later, in the middle of the day, I monitored a radio message that Mike Stone was known to be wanted and he was in Stall Street selling papers. The warning went out not to approach him until we had got three or four officers gathered.

I called up on the radio saying that, as I knew this man, I would make my way back into the centre and no one was to take any action until I had spoken with him. The radio operator accepted my direction. I drove into the centre and walked up to him, greeting him as I would a friend. I told him he was wanted and I needed him to come to the police station with me. His response was, 'Okay, Mr Hale', and together we made our way to the custody unit. Again, proof, if proof were needed, that the spoken word often is less painful than struggling on the ground making an arrest.

Back to the psychiatric unit. Another regular at Hillview was a lady we will call Pru, a well-known drug user. Often the staff would summon me when they had a problem and if some damage was caused by a patient; I used to think that it was in the hope that I might arrest and remove the patient. Wrong. No custody sergeant would accept a prisoner arrested from a psychiatric unit. On this particular evening, I was called by a psychiatrist, and when I arrived he told me that Pru would not take her medication and had broken something. He then told me that she was in the smoking room. So along we both went to see her. As we entered the room, she was sitting smoking, so I sat down next to her.

'What's the problem then, Pru? Why won't you take your medicine?'

There was no reply but there was a response. She reached across with the hand holding the cigarette and started to stub it out on my thigh. I grabbed her arm and asked the psychiatrist whether she was a sectioned patient and he said no. 'In that case,' I told him, 'she is now leaving.' I told him to find a black bag and we went to her room. The psychiatrist packed up her stuff and I walked her to the exit. As we approached the door, I think the reality of the situation struck home and despite her wishes to stay I ejected her.

It did not take long before the control room contacted me to ask whether I had just thrown a patient out of the hospital, because a friend of hers was on the phone. I confirmed that I had. Pru, of course, knew how to play the system because within about forty hours she was back in the ward. I was talking to a male nurse when I next saw Pru down the corridor. I signalled to her to come to me, which she did. I then said to her in full hearing of the nurse, 'Pru, if you ever do that again, I shall punch you right in the nose. Now push off!' She never said a word but waddled away.

'I wish *we* could talk to them like that,' said the nurse. Obviously, it was a hollow threat but she never caused me anymore trouble.

Knowing your community

Having knowledge of many of the patients, particularly those who were residents in the homes, was at times beneficial. One such time was when I was sent to a flat in Newbridge Road to see a very distressed student who had been waiting at a bus stop in the dark when she was approached by a man who had started talking to her and would not go away. Thankfully, the student had two flatmates, who she had returned to and who had calmed her down somewhat but were nonetheless fearful of the incident that had occurred.

I started to take an account of what had happened and gained a description from her. She gave a good description, then I asked what he had said. She said he had told her he had been to The Pavilion for some entertainment that evening and was on his way home. She told me that, despite not engaging to any great degree, he would not go away. Then she said, 'He asked me if he could be my boyfriend', and when she said that, a light bulb switched on in my mind.

It had to be Peter (not his real name), who was a resident in one of the psychiatric homes, as he was frequently seeking a 'girlfriend'. I rang the home and asked whether Peter had been out that evening, and the answer was yes. I was told that he had gone down into the city. I then asked what he had been wearing, and when I got the answer, it matched entirely.

When I explained to the young lady who the man who had approached her was, and his circumstances, she was most forgiving and understanding and wanted no more action taken. The value of local knowledge; it saved a great deal of time perhaps searching the area and it also meant that there and then the complainant's mind was set at ease.

Building up a relationship with Hillview Lodge also worked in other odd ways. One of the patients on the unit, a young woman, had reported to the police that she had been raped. However, when a statement was required, which would normally have been taken by a policewoman, the young lady said she would only give her statement to me. It took a couple of sessions putting this together but I am assuming she had trust in me as someone she knew. Ultimately, it did not go anywhere and the veracity of the claim probably did not stand up to too much close examination. Again, though, the value of knowing your community and being accepted into it.

Smile, please

I never thought I would be a pin-up, but I became so on one of the psychiatric wards during my time.

There had been a spate of criminal damage to garden walls around our neighbourhood and one evening I was half asleep on the couch, dressed only in my dressing gown, when I was woken up by the sound of masonry being knocked over. I leapt up, shouted for Jane to dial 999 and ran out of the house barefoot to see a group of youths kicking over a wall two houses up from me. As I approached, they ran off, and I continued in a somewhat painful pursuit over bits of broken pavement and odd stones. They cut through a garage block and I ran around the main road to see them come out the other side and split up. The nearest one, who was about 12 or 13, ran across the road, having gone down a steep grass bank. I managed successfully to negotiate the bank without slipping over and then catch up with him, he on one side of a hedge and me on the other. Having now told him I was a police officer, he eventually gave up and I arrested him and led him back to our road as I heard the sound of sirens approaching. The officers took the lad from me. It seemed most odd that no one had reported a mature man, dressed only in a dressing gown and barefoot, chasing a schoolboy around the street! What was even odder was that I made my way towards my home but stopped to speak to one of the householders who had lost their wall, and while engaged in conversation, I saw a small group of lads reappear from a lane and they matched those I had seen earlier, so I walked up to them and arrested them as well, and the car came back to take them off to the police station.

The following day I received a call from the press telling me that the police PR officer had sent out the story and could they have a photo. The *Evening Post* photographer came to my home and also asked my neighbour if I could sit on their wall, which had been destroyed. 'Oh, and by the way, can you get undressed and put your dressing gown on?' A photograph was taken. The next time I went into the ward office at Hillview there was much giggling, and there on the office wall was a full colour photograph cut out from the papers.

Me posing on the broken wall.
(Mirrorpix)

The Horse

I talked about death earlier and mentioned the pain of losing a dog. On a quiet Sunday afternoon I was in a panda car on my beat when there was a call regarding a traffic collision beyond Corston, to the west of Bath, on the A39. The report stated that a car had hit a horse and rider and the horse had run off injured. I said I would make my way towards the incident and reached the village of Corston, where at the junction of the main road and the road into the village centre stood a lady. I stopped and asked if she had seen an injured horse. She told me she had and that it was a little way into the village. I drove into the centre of the village and there was the horse standing with its rear offside lower leg hanging by one or two sinews. I immediately asked for a vet and then went over to the horse, which was being held by its reins by a couple of people, but it was still trying to move forward. My equestrian course with the police was of value because, while I respect horses, I do not fear them. Because it was trying to move forward, I went in front of it and put my arms around its neck and my head towards its head, leaning forward into it. Then I started talking to it to try to calm it. Initially, the radio operator told me they were having problems getting a vet. Again, local knowledge of my beat enabled me to tell them where there was a vet and I asked for a car to go there and escort him to the scene, remembering to tell them not to use the sirens on approach, which might well have spooked the horse. An age passed as I continued to talk to the horse, and then when the vet did eventually arrive, there seemed no sense of urgency and I shouted over to him, 'Doc, can you please hurry up.'

Eventually, he came to the horse and, while I still held it, injected fluid into its neck. It was fast acting, causing me to have to jump clear as the poor beast fell to the floor. I had only been talking to it for twenty minutes but it was enough to bring me to the verge of tears as it fell.

I am an examiner for the Institute of Advanced Motorists and the odd sequel to this, many years later, was that I went to Shepton Mallet to conduct a driver assessment. These are provided to allow a motorist to have their driving assessed. On this occasion it was a young lady, and while we were going around, I asked what had prompted her to seek an assessment. She explained that she was a nervous driver and that she had had a nasty accident as a learner near Corston once.

'Was it on a Sunday?' I asked her.

'Yes,' was her reply.

'Did it involve a horse?' I continued, and again her answer was affirmative. How on earth did I know that? she enquired. I then explained that I had in fact dealt with the injured horse. They talk about rounding the circle, don't they!

A number of thank-you letters came in thanking me for my work that Sunday afternoon).

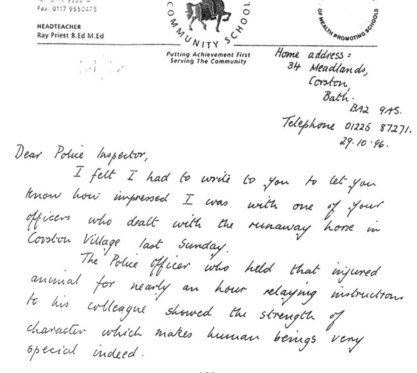

Bristol BS5 9JH
Tel. 0117 9553141
Fax. 0117 9550475

HEADTEACHER
Ray Priest B.Ed M.Ed

Putting Achievement First
Serving The Community

Home address =
34 Meadlands,
Corston,
Bath.
BA2 9AS.
Telephone 01225 87271.
29.10.96.

Dear Police Inspector,

I felt I had to write to you to let you know how impressed I was with one of your officers who dealt with the runaway horse in Corston Village last Sunday.

The Police Officer who held that injured animal for nearly an hour relaying instructions to his colleague showed the strength of character which makes human beings very special indeed.

It took not only physical strength, because this huge animal was distressed and trying to bolt on three legs with its remaining leg hanging by a thread (but) but also moral fibre as the policeman comforted the young owner and organised the people trying to contain the situation.

It was clear to me that the police officer was himself moved by the sadness of it all.

Please thank him and the other young policeman. They were both magnificent at all times even to ensuring that the vet followed procedures.

Sent with respects.

Julie Miller.

Teacher at above school & wife to the Clerk of the Village Council.

Not Me, Guv

It was an evening shift, probably around midnight, when I received a call to a smashed window in a shop at the bottom of Chelsea Road, on my patch. I was on foot and the walk to the scene took me perhaps ten minutes or so. On arrival I saw the shop window smashed, and sitting on a wall opposite were a couple of the local low-lives – one in particular – so I had a word with them and one told me that the window had been like that when they had come to sit on the wall.

I then left them and went to the flat of the informant, on the other side of Newbridge Road, which overlooked the scene. When she opened the door, her opening words were, 'He didn't tell you he didn't do it, did he?'

'Yes," I said.

'Well, it was definitely him; I watched him do it.'

I went back to the pair and arrested the more well-known low-life she had identified – well known because I frequently dealt with him for stupid things. He was charged with criminal damage and we went to court, where he pleaded not guilty. I was called to the witness box to face a sometimes typically arrogant legal-aid defence lawyer. He led me through the story, doing his best to trip me up, and then he reached the point where he asked me whether I really thought his client would have committed this crime and remained there. I reminded him of the testimony of the witness who placed him as the offender.

Not content with this, he persisted and asked me whether I really expected the court to believe that having committed this crime, his client would be content to remain there. He had opened the door for me, and my response was, 'Yes, I do, and I am on oath. If you knew your client as well as I do, you would believe it because your client –' At this point there was a very hasty interruption by the defence solicitor: 'Yes, thank you, officer. I have no further questions.' And with that, his client was found guilty. There are times when solicitors can be as stupid as their clients.

The Value of School Visits

From time to time I would visit the primary schools on my beat and talk to them about various topics: perhaps about keeping themselves safe, stranger danger and other odds and ends. The nice thing was that it meant the children would hopefully see the police officer as a person and someone they could talk to. When I entered the playground at break time, it was like bees around a honey pot, just a sea of little people, with some wrapping their arms around my thigh and me thinking this perhaps should not be happening!

The nice outcome was that on the street I would hear a small voice call across the road saying, 'Hello, Alan', and I think achieving this was a success. I was quite happy to be called Alan because they could have called me a lot worse!

One evening I was patrolling in a car when I received a call on the radio, the operator saying, 'We have taken a 999 call from what sounds like a child, saying, "Daddy has taken some tablets and we can't wake him up."' I was only half a mile away, so I said I would attend, and as luck had it I was the first to arrive. I got out of the car, walked to the front door and rang the bell. The front door opened and at first glance there appeared to be no one there, until I looked down, and there, holding the door, was a little tot who looked up at me and said, 'Hello, PC Hale.' To me, this was fantastic; not because it was me, but because this little child had sensibly rung the police and then, in her hour of most desperate need and at such a young age, had opened the door to a face she knew rather than that of a stranger. A very positive spin-off from school visits.

The Bike

Me on the pedal cycle.
(Mirrorpix)

Having a foot-patrol beat is lovely, but occasionally it can be a long walk from one end to the other. So what is the answer? Well, a pedal cycle was what I thought. There was a new cycle shop just off my patch, so a visit there one day and a chat with the owner eventually yielded a brand-new cycle presented to the police for my use. It was far better than the ones we used when I had started out in Bristol. The downside, of course, was that, unlike the old black heavy metal Raleigh bikes of my earlier days, the cycle I was now using was much more attractive to thieves and so, perhaps not sur-prisingly, had to be locked wherever I left it.

The result was that it became more of a hindrance than a help.

The Bus

We had the privilege of free bus travel, so on suitable shifts I would travel from home to Bath on the bus. I think it gave the driver confidence, and also the passengers, as I always travelled in uniform to and fro. It was just a case of showing your warrant card if you were not in uniform. It also enabled me to travel out to my beat from the station if I decided not to walk, though for the most part I walked.

One summer's afternoon I had boarded the bus at home and it was a quiet, uneventful journey until we approached the end of the dual carriageway on the A4, known as the Twerton Straight. At this point I glanced out of the nearside windows across the adjacent field, and there, stood in full view, was a young man with his coat open, exposing himself indecently to any passing traffic. 'Stop the bus,' I said to the driver, and he pulled in. 'Stay here, please' was my parting request as I left the bus and climbed over the boundary wall. Initially, the young man did not see me, but as I got nearer he noticed me and quickly pulled his coat together.

When asked what he thought he was doing, he told me he was doing nothing. I asked him to open his coat and, of course, when he did the evidence was there, plainly to be seen. In addition to that, he had a length of baling twine tied around each thigh. Why? Well, this kept his trousers up, so that with his coat closed his trousers looked normal and with his coat open he had his hands free, with no danger of his trousers falling around his ankles.

I arrested him, put him in handcuffs and then walked him back to the roadside, where the bus driver was still patiently waiting. We boarded the bus and were taken to the bus station, from where I walked my prisoner across to the nearby police station.

A simple arrest, but one that took me almost the whole of my shift: paperwork and then the interview, after we had waited a number of hours for his solicitor, who then wanted to be shown the scene of the crime, so out we went. I do not recall whether he ever went to court but at least no one was offended by him, or no one who made a complaint!

Our Policeman

It seems to me that community policing is all about being known in your community and hopefully being respected. If you can achieve that, the community, to a great level, take possession of you and also take care of you, as is shown in the next couple of recollections.

On a sunny afternoon I was sent to a domestic dispute at a house at the bottom end of Newbridge Hill, just below Chelsea Road. The complainant was a lady who lived with her daughter but also had a man friend, and it seemed that the relationship had come to an end and she wanted him out of the house.

Upon arrival the verbally violent argument was still in full swing and the lady was outside the front door. While I was talking to her, the man came out in a rage and, despite being asked to leave, would not calm down. I told him he risked arrest but this did not help. He made threats and the woman retreated to the house, and though I tried to stop him, he followed her. I then decided to arrest him and, on the radio, called 10.9, which is the code for immediate assistance. However, in Bath there were never more than three cars out, normally only two, so whoever came would be doing their best, but they would not drop out of the sky!

Having made the call, I then went into the house to find that mother and daughter had locked themselves in the front, ground-floor room. However, between them and me was the man friend, who had ripped a length of timber with metal coat hooks on it from the hall wall and was trying to break down the door with it. I decided I had to take a chance that the troops would not be long and closed with the man and managed to disarm him. Following a struggle, I managed to get behind him and pin his arms at his side while dragging him into the kitchen and forcing him against a kitchen unit, thus containing him between it and me. Fine, but there was absolutely nothing I could do with him without endangering myself, so I decided to hold him in containment until my assistance arrived. The kitchen door had closed behind us, but within four or five minutes there was a knock and it opened slowly. A couple of men I did not know peered around the door and asked if they could help. Relief. I indicated with my head towards my handcuffs and asked them to take them off my belt and put them on one arm, which they did, and then we managed to get the other arm locked in. A short while later my official assistance arrived outside.

So who were these men who had come to my aid? Well, upon hearing the commotion and the attempts to smash his way into the living room, the daughter had climbed out of the front window and run to the pub on the corner of Chelsea Road, arriving in a state, asking to use the phone to dial 999. When asked why, she explained that 'the local policeman' was fighting with the man and was on his own. Once she had explained, two customers immediately left the pub and came to my rescue. I was extremely grateful because I am not sure how much longer I could have held him.

This was not the only time the public rose to the challenge.

One winter's evening, I attended a report of noisy and disorderly youths at Charmouth Road, Newbridge. Upon arrival there were about six or seven teenagers with a local girl from the road. Attempts to get them to be quiet met with the usual abuse. The lads were from over the river in Twerton. My first action was to send the girl home, with threats of coming to speak with her parents later. She went. I then tried to shepherd the lads towards the main road, still receiving lots of mouth. I became aware of a man leaving a house a little way behind me and walking towards me. As he approached one of the lads said, 'Aye, mate, you got a pen? I want to take his number to complain about him.'

The man answered, 'Yes, I have a pen.'

'Can I borrow it, mate?'

The man answered, 'No, because in a minute *my* policeman may want me to write something down for him.'

Then I heard another front door shut further up the road, and when I looked around there was another man walking toward us zipping up his jacket. Both men were probably in their fifties. He came up to us, and together the three of us shepherded them out of Charmouth Road and into Newbridge Road. Once on the main road I thanked both of the men for their assistance. Then, as they walked away, moments later a car heading into Bath pulled up by my side and the nearside window was wound down. The driver called out, 'Do you need any assistance, officer?' It was as though I had died and gone to heaven, where every member of the community helped the police. It really was extremely reassuring knowing that there were those on my community beat who had my back in times of need. Very brave men.

Bath Asian Council

A lovely lady called Usha Kumar, who as I recall was a social worker, lived on my patch, and her husband ran a corner shop.

At that time, I believe Usha was the chairwoman of the Bath Asian Council, and as such invited me along to an event. Well, their events almost invariably involved food, and the food was prepared and presented by the women. It was fantastic. It was really nice to support them, and a little while later I convinced the powers that be at the station that they should pay for me to become a full member, which they did.

It was very rewarding being a part of such a cultural group. As a result of my involvement I was invited to be the main speaker at a large fundraising event in Bristol – an after-dinner speaker, as of course there was food again! I asked what the dress code was and was told evening dress. I also asked whether Jane and I could bring another couple, and this was agreed. So the four of us, dressed smartly in our black-tie outfits, arrived only to find all the women in very colourful, smart saris and their men in smart-casual attire. Thankfully, Dave and Dawn were with Jane and I, so at least we were not alone in our dress code!

The Winner of the Ray Robinson Trophy

Doing the job was always a great pleasure, and as they say, if I could have afforded it, I would have done it for nothing. I have always described it as a paid hobby. That said, it is, of course, nice to be appreciated, and so it was when I was nominated for and chosen to receive the Ray Robinson Trophy 1994. The Ray Robinson Trophy is awarded annually to the police officer, or group of officers, believed to have made the greatest contribution to community relations outside of the greater Bristol area.

Ray Robinson retired from Avon and Somerset Police in 1978 due to ill health. From his retirement until he passed away, Ray worked tirelessly within the community, especially with those who were mentally handicapped. I was privileged to receive the award personally from Ray in 1994. It was nice that my wife and daughters were able to attend the presentation at Taunton, as indeed were a large number of friends and associates from my community beat.

Receiving the Ray Robinson Trophy from the man himself (in the foreground) at the ceremony at Canonsgrove Training Centre, Taunton. From the left: Sarah (who blinked at the wrong moment), Jane, Clare and me.

The Royal United Hospital Children's Ward

It is always sad to witness children having to be in-patients in any hospital, but equally it was always a pleasure to be able to do something positive, and visits in uniform seemed to achieve smiles and interactions. Only on one occasion did a little black lad tell me, 'I don't like coppers!' That told me I had some 'hearts and minds' work to do there.

The staff were all marvelous with the children, and they also had the skill of making me a great cup of tea, as indeed did many other wards and departments.

On one of my first Christmases covering the ward I thought it might be nice to be Father Christmas for the patients. The security team at the hospital told me they had a sleigh that could be used.

The ward opened onto a large, flat-roofed balcony, which overlooked the neighbouring cricket field where the air ambulance used to land for A & E seriously ill patient delivery. In the centre of Bath I visited a theatrical-costume-hire shop, which agreed to provide a full Father Christmas outfit and properly deal with my make-up, stuck-on beard, white bushy eyebrows and rosy red cheeks.

This left only one question: how would I arrive at the hospital? So in for a penny, in for a pound. A telephone call to Wiltshire Police Helicopter Unit was made and they were more than willing to collect me from a playing field at Penn Hill and fly me into the cricket field while all the children on the ward gathered on the flat roof.

So it was, that one lunchtime towards Christmas, I went to the shop and, as promised, they carried out a very professional make-up job. I was then driven to the playing field by Sergeant Mike Stanton, the community sergeant, a lovely dedicated policeman. I had already armed myself with a large handbell provided by the security team, part of the set with the sleigh. A little later the helicopter came over the hill and landed and I climbed into the rear seat with the bell on my lap. As I moved to fasten my belt, my knees parted and the bell fell through, just missing one of the floor-mounted TV screens for the operational camera. This could have been a very expensive short flight and, no doubt, a lot of writing for someone.

It was a fantastic, although short, flight. We did a bit of a fly-past to begin with, me waving to a roof full of excited kids who were waving back. We then circled and landed and I climbed out to be welcomed by Senior Staff Nurse Jenny Mackenzie and a student nurse from the children's ward. The *Bath Chronicle* had sent a photographer to capture the arrival.

I was then escorted to the pedestrian entrance of A & E, where I was met by my pair of elves, dressed as security men, ready with the sleigh, which I dutifully entered. I was then towed through A & E and Outpatients and into the corridor to the lift. Along the way I greeted everyone we passed, many of whom I would talk with during the normal course of a day, but they showed no recognition at all that the jolly man in the red suit was in fact me.

Arriving on the ward, I was surrounded by excited children and spent much time with them, talking and listening to what they wanted for Christmas. Among the children was the young black lad. When I asked him what he wanted for Christmas, he looked straight at me and said, 'You're not Father Christmas.'

'Oh yes I am,' I replied.

'You're not.'

'I am.'

'No you're not. You're the policeman.'

A very astute young lad, and Father Christmas then moved on!

From left to right: Senior Staff Nurse Jenny Mackenzie, me and a student nurse from the children's ward.
(Mirrorpix)

The Heart Attack

Walking around my beat and talking with people was a big part of the job, and one Sunday morning I was passing along Cedric Road when up ahead I saw an elderly lady leaning on her front gate.

When I reached her, I greeted her with a 'Good morning and how are you?'. She responded positively and a conversation started, which took in a number of topics and went on for some ten minutes or more. Then, almost as an afterthought, she said, 'What should you do if someone is having a heart attack?'

'Who is having the heart attack?' I asked.

'It's my husband.'

'Where is he?' I asked with more urgency now.

'He is in the house!'

I very quickly ushered her back into the house and into the rear sitting room. Sure enough, her husband was sitting there in a chair in some discomfort but not presenting as though he was suffering a heart attack. I then helped her contact the GP!

Thinking About Retirement

As 1996 dawned, the start of the last six months of my thirty years' service began. I was seeking a job to retire into; we still had a mortgage, so a job was necessary. You start off by believing that you have a lot to offer the outside world but that thought is soon undermined. Many applications but limited interviews achieved. There was one job that I thought I should have a good chance at, having been a Traffic motorcyclist and a live traffic broadcaster on the two local radio stations. The AA were advertising for a motorcyclist to patrol traffic routes and give live broadcasts on the state of the traffic back to the radio station. I did not even get an interview for that. I had an interview for a job with Bath Building Society but was not successful. I applied for the position of first line manager for the reception team at A & E at the Royal United Hospital but again without success. I also applied for the post of Coroner's Officer for Bristol but forgot the fact that the role also covered Treasure Trove and could not answer the question when asked in interview.

What I did not want to apply for were jobs in security, though had the role of security manager at the RUH come up, I would have jumped at the chance.

Eventually, though, I had to consider security roles and applied for the post of security manager for a long-established department store in Bath. I was invited for an initial interview by the store manager. She put me at ease and then asked me to give an account of my background and experience, which I did with confidence. Once finished, she said, 'Well, clearly this is just the job for you.'

I replied, 'Well, not really. I did not want to go into security work, but everyone told me I should give it a go, so here I am.'

On the strength of that interview and that honest answer, I was invited for a formal interview with the national or regional security manager. On the day, I turned up at the store and was shown into a small room to wait. After a short period of time a head appeared around the door. 'Mr Hale? I'm Mr Rogers.' And with that the head disappeared. I assumed I was supposed to follow him, so I did. He disappeared into a room and I followed. Once in, he told me where I was to sit. It was then that I probably put an end to any prospects by offering my hand and saying 'Good afternoon'. Oh! 'Good afternoon' was the begrudging reply. Clearly, the room had not been prepared for interview, as it was untidy, and partway through, the telephone at the other end of the room started to ring and he broke off to answer it. Thankfully, I never received an offer!

After almost a year of trying various avenues, I was offered a post as a trainee emergency medical technician with Wings, a private ambulance company. The downside was that it was still shift work. I was sent to the NHS Ambulance Training Centre in Chippenham on a six-week course. There were only six of us on the course, and the other five were from the Oxfordshire Ambulance Service and were at best twenty years younger than me; only one of them ever entered into conversation with me. It was hard work for six weeks, and quite a lonely course as well. Despite all of that, I qualified as an emergency medical technician.

On joining the team at Wings, Andy was my mentor. Apparently, there had been a widespread reluctance to be crewed with a retired policeman! I tried hard to refer to the force as 'the police' rather than as something I was still part of.

The role took me all over the southern half of the country

delivering patients to private hospitals or transferring them from one hospital to another. A big part of the company's business was holiday retrievals, collecting people from the airport and taking them home or to a hospital.

During the first week, Andy and I were sent to Heathrow to collect a patient who had a blocked urinary tract and was coming off a flight. As Andy was the qualified man, it was appropriate that he should do the nursing bit in the back with a doctor and probably one of the Wings' flight nurses. I had the patient's wife up front with me. Why we could not take him straight to a local hospital for the necessary treatment, I do not know, but the orders were to take him to a hospital in his home town of Nuneaton, a journey of just over a hundred miles – all conducted on blue lights and sirens. So that really was fun!

Another incident that stands out in my mind was one afternoon when I was working with a female emergency medical technician. We were heading for Chippenham, along the A420, and were about a half mile short of Marshfield. I was the passenger. A view opened up ahead across drystone walls and my colleague decided to take the opportunity to overtake the vehicle in front. I can only imagine that, despite looking in her mirror, a BMW saloon was in her blind spot and travelling at high speed. It is odd how things happen in slow motion, because I saw the BMW pass us, but by now on the offside verge, and collide with a drystone wall on the offside, which catapulted the car across the road in front of us. I watched the car fly across the height of the windscreen before passing over the drystone wall on my nearside and crash land in the field, turning over a few times before coming to rest. We quickly came to a halt and my colleague jumped out to go to the car while I took to the radio to ask the office to summon a mainstream NHS ambulance to the crash. I then went to the field, where the driver had either got out or had been pulled out and was lying on the ground. He seemed quiet until I got there, at which point he started shouting at me and calling me all the names imaginable, until my colleague informed him that I had not been the driver but she had.

The NHS ambulance arrived with a spinal board, and the crew started to tend to the driver, putting him on the spinal board and strapping him on firmly to protect against any spinal issues. Throughout, he was being rude and protesting, and when they got him into the ambulance, he fought to get off the board. He was conveyed by them to the Royal United Hospital, where later we found out he had discharged himself. Once the NHS ambulance had left, we got back into our ambulance, where my colleague broke down in tears. She was clearly shocked, so I took us, in our ambulance, to a tea shop in Marshfield to help her settle down.

The job lasted for about eighteen months, until Avon Ambulance Service offered me a post on their Patient Transport Service, working days, with weekends off. Lovely people to work with but the service itself gave me the worst year of my working life. They were so petty, and officers with pips on their shoulders seemed reluctant to take responsibility.

Two occasions stand out, one when I had a dental appointment mid afternoon so I said to one of the officers, 'When I come out of the dentist, there will only be an hour of duty left. Do you want me to come back and sit in the station or shall I just go home?' The pragmatic answer would have been to just go home. That was sort of the answer, but he told me that if anyone asked me, I should tell them I did not come out of the dentist until the end of my duty – so, in other words, lie about it!

On another occasion, I had a young female probationary trainee paramedic with me. We came upon a road traffic collision in Westbury-on-Trym, where an elderly lady had been struck on a zebra crossing by a car. It was raining and she lay in the road. She wanted to try to get up and go on her way. Clearly not ideal. A front-line ambulance had been called but had not arrived. I decided I needed to calm the casualty down and try to retain her dignity. We needed to move her off the road, so I sent my colleague to get our stretcher. Following the extensive training I had undergone when I had qualified as an NHS standard emergency medical technician, I established from witnesses the dynamics of the collision and that it had not been high speed. I then carried out a survey of the lady, checking for any obvious fractures, and found nothing. With the stretcher to hand, and with the aid of bystanders, we lifted her onto the stretcher and covered her for warmth. My actions settled the casualty down. Having done this, the ambulance arrived, crewed by an ambulance woman and an ambulance officer bearing pips. I told him what had happened, what I had done, and I suggested that she remain on our stretcher and we would come to the hospital to collect it.

Nothing was said. They each took one end of the stretcher and moved to the ambulance. Now, I had been trained to stand either side to lift and feed the stretcher into the back of the ambulance to guard against slipping. They chose to do it the other way, and what happened? The ambulance woman went first and her legs buckled under her as she climbed up the steps under the weight of the stretcher. Thankfully, my colleague and I were there and were able to prevent a professional catastrophe by catching the stretcher and bearing some of the weight.

A day or so later I heard, over the radio, my colleague of that evening incident being recalled to ambulance HQ in Bristol to see the training officer. Surprise, surprise, I was then called back. Fortunately, I returned in time to speak to my colleague and assure her that if asked about it, she should tell the training officer it was my decisions that led to the action we took. I did not want to, in any way, adversely affect her future career.

After a little while I was summoned to the officer's office, where she started by asking me whether I had forgotten the bit in my training that talks about not moving casualties. I then told her the full circumstances: that I had established the mechanism of injury and that, following my training as an emergency medical technician, I had assessed the casualty and, by lifting her onto the stretcher, had calmed her and made her safe. I then asked why, if I had done wrong, had the ambulance officer at the scene not reprimand me, neither at the scene nor at the hospital, where we had exchanged stretchers? He had said nothing, clearly preferring to run behind my back to the training officer. She was quite surprised and asked me to confirm that nothing had been said by the officer, which I did. I also mentioned the problem of the stretcher nearly being dropped due to not following training guidelines! Surprisingly, neither I nor my colleague heard any more about it. I suspect the officer might have received words of advice.

Avon Ambulance at that time had a planning team, who each day put together the collection run sheets for the following day's runs. Each morning the crews would come on duty, pick up their run sheets and sit there for half an hour rearranging the sheets into a workable order. This was happening at every ambulance station in Avon.

After a while I managed to secure a posting to Keynsham Ambulance Station as one of the two-man crew whose primary task was to serve the general hospital's day clinics. This was steady work, and Eddie, the long-standing crew member, was a great guy to work with.

I continued to look for a different job and was successful in becoming a planning enforcement officer with Bath and North East Somerset Council. Not long after I was employed I became a shop steward for the Planning Department. The then branch secretary and chairman both stood down together, I think to prove a point about something, no doubt expecting the branch to speak highly of them and ask them to return. They didn't, and so I became the

Unison union branch secretary. I became the secretary about a month before there was a national strike about pensions, as I recall. As secretary I really had no choice other than to go on strike for the day, much as I disagree with the worth of strike action.

It was a good role and I had a lovely assistant called Molly, who had been used as little more than a typist by the previous secretary. The first thing I told Molly to do was to contact her peers in the neighbouring councils and find out what they were being paid. The result showed that Molly had been kept on a below-average wage by my predecessor. So Molly and I had a discussion and we came to an agreed settlement, which was that the branch would pay Molly a significant lump sum there and then for the money withheld from her and her hourly pay would be raised by a good amount. I also made her office manager and gave her the power to take certain decisions in my absence. Molly was a great person to work with and we shared a peculiar sense of humour, which made work more fun. (See my character reference from Molly later in the book.)

The role of a planning enforcement officer, while somewhat mundane, had its moments of challenge, but the one that stands out in my mind was not directly connected with Planning. One lunchtime I was sitting in the office when I took a call from Morgan Baynham, another planning enforcement officer, also a retired police officer. Morgan asked me if I could come downstairs, as he was watching a man acting suspiciously in the rear yard. I ran downstairs and out into the yard, and there was a man apparently secreting something in a planter. Morgan then appeared from the building.

I challenged the man and he started walking away towards the city centre. However, I went after him and he turned around and came back to the planter, grabbed some property from where he had hidden it and then started to run, so we set off in lukewarm pursuit. Morgan was clearly more of an athlete than me and led the pursuit as we entered Queen Square. Not being a great fan of running, I leapt out into the traffic and stopped a pickup truck, asking the driver to 'follow that man up there' while pointing out the pursued. Amazingly, he did, and we overtook Morgan, but the other guy had disappeared. I asked my driver to stop and I leapt out, now ahead of Morgan, who later revealed that he did not know how that had happened. I asked a man near the rear of a building whether he had seen someone running, and he said he had and pointed us in the right direction.

We came out on Charlotte Street, at the then register office. Morgan had already rung 999 on his mobile. As we stood there, the man appeared from the rear of the building, saying that he had got rid of the stuff, so no need to worry. Well, having been forced to run, even a bit, I was in no mood to just leave it. I grabbed the offender around the neck, saying that I was making a citizen's arrest, and dragged him to the floor. In the process he bit me on the bicep. He struggled violently, and while I held him in a neck hold, Morgan held his torso down and we both called 999 on our mobiles. The operator did not seem to know where Queen Square, Bath, was and I told her we were both retired police officers and needed immediate assistance. The commotion continued and a piano delivery van pulled up. The driver jumped out, asking whether we needed assistance, so I told him to stand on the felon's legs, which he did. Eventually, a police car turned up, crewed by two very diminutive policewomen. After a struggle, we helped them put the man into handcuffs. During all of this an ambulance also turned up; the people upstairs in the adjacent building had heard the commotion, looked out and had thought there had been a road traffic collision, so had summoned an ambulance!

The criminal was eventually sent to prison, but I had a worrying time for a while; as he was a drug addict, and because he had sunk his teeth into me and drawn blood, I had to attend the hospital for tests, which thankfully eventually proved to be negative.

The planning enforcement job lasted for two years, but then in 2003 I achieved my dream non-police job. After a competitive interview, I became the senior road safety officer for South Gloucestershire Council. I was responsible for road-safety education and training in whatever format was necessary. I also had some forty to fifty school crossing patrols and was at the point of starting a couple of casual cycle training coordinators. I also inherited one road safety officer, who chose to concentrate solely on the school crossing patrols and finished work at 4 pm on the dot.

Thankfully, within a month of me starting, we employed a fantastic lady, Pam Williams, as an assistant road safety officer. Pam had been the road safety officer for Windsor and Maidenhead but had been commuting from her home, not far from Bath, to Windsor. Pam filled the void that existed in the support I needed, and together, over time, we developed a fantastic team. My inherited road safety officer was signed off sick with 'work-related stress' for six months prior to the day of her retirement. In the local authority full pay is provided for sick leave up to six months.

Within perhaps four years or so we had developed a Bikeability cycle training team (the much-improved replacement for Cycle Proficiency) of some twenty cycle trainers, plus two or three training coordinators and a cycle training manager and a new assistant road safety officer, as Pam was now road safety officer and my number two. We also had a motorcycle officer and a technical support officer for the cycle training team, three road safety assistants and a school travel plan officer.

We were a great team, a very successful one, and nationally we were the safest local authority in the country for one or two years and the second safest another year, behind the Isles of Sicily (so first really!).

Considering that I had worked outside for most of my working life, I was surprised that, having to be in the office more and more, I was not climbing the walls!

In the late 2000s South Gloucestershire Council carried out some reorganisation to cut costs, but I managed to ensure that my team was not affected. However, around 2014 there was to be another reorganisation to save even more money. I decided that there was a real chance that my team would suffer. In order to try to guard against this, I put together a reorganisation plan for my team, such that four people would step up a grade and I would take myself out of the equation on voluntary redundancy. My plan was accepted and thankfully no one else in the team lost their job.

Councillor Alan Hale

In 2007 I was selected to stand as a Conservative district councillor for Keynsham South on Bath and North East Somerset Council. At that time the ward was a two-seat ward, and both were then Labour. I worked very hard and called on every door on the ward, and in May 2007 I succeeded, coming in second and gaining one of the two seats. I think that most votes were personal ones. As I had lived on the council estate, and on the doorstep, many told me that they had worked with my mum at the hospital or used to drink with my dad at the Wingrove pub. I was also quite well known in the community because of my membership and work within the Lions Club of Keynsham. As I continue to write this now, in 2022, I have had the privilege of being returned on three further occasions and hope that in 2023 I shall be successful again.

In 2016 I was elected as chairman of the council and had a fantastic year. Jane and I were privileged to attend a Royal Garden Party at Buckingham Palace. We enjoyed the gardens and the tea, after which we were all summoned to be arranged into avenues for the royals to walk down and talk to people. Having been so arranged, Jane decided she needed the toilet! The facilities were the other side of the avenue of people opposite. Jane set off, with me thinking that she would never get back in time. How wrong I was.

Jane is a quiet person, but there, opposite, was my wife, elbowing her way through the gathered crowd in time to run back across the avenue to me before Her Majesty The Queen, may she rest in peace, arrived in front of us.

As the chair of council, I met and shook hands with many 'A' listers, as they say. The list of handshakes included HRH Camilla Duchess of Cornwall, now queen consort. When she had visited St John's Hospital charity and residential homes in the middle of Bath, I was part of the welcoming line-up. Her Royal Highness seemed to me to be a very down-to-earth person, a nice person, who clearly makes the then Prince Charles happy – which he deserves. With the sad passing of the late queen, Camilla has become queen consort and Prince Charles is now king.

The Chancellor of the University of Bath was and still is, in 2022, Prince Edward, Duke of Wessex, and again I was part of the welcoming line-up, accompanied by Jane. Later that morning I hosted him at lunch at the Guildhall. While in that particular line-up, and awaiting the duke's arrival, I noticed Sir Bobby Charlton coming from the robing room. He had, earlier that morning, been awarded an honorary doctorate. I am not a football-mad person, but Sir Bobby is, I believe, an old-school gentleman and an outstanding star footballer, and I could not allow myself to miss the chance to meet him, shake his hand and just say hello. It was a very short exchange but what a nice man.

At a large Christian event in the Guildhall, Justin Welby, Archbishop of Canterbury, had been invited and I had been asked, as council chairman, to welcome him at the door and, at the end of the event, offer the vote of thanks to him. I remember saying in my speech of thanks that when I had come to the Christian faith ten years earlier (and that gained an enthusiastic round of applause), I never thought that ten years later I would be meeting, thanking and shaking hands with the Archbishop of Canterbury. I joked that he had moved above Sir Bobby Charlton in my list of handshakes.

He responded by saying that he would have kept Sir Bobby on top!

Actor Jeremy Irons was installed as Chancellor of Bath Spa University, and again I attended that ceremony and spent time chatting with him beforehand. What amused me was that he was taken onto the dais in Bath Abbey, to be installed, and I was placed in the front row. I was a great fan of Happy Socks multi-coloured creations and I wore them on my official engagements. Jane did not like them, but when Jeremy Irons sat down and crossed his legs, he displayed a green sock on one foot and a red sock on the other, so my colourful socks were clearly okay.

Finally, at another university event, I was able to meet and shake hands with radio and TV presenter, the late Bill Turnbull. A perfect gentleman.

After my second full council meeting as chairman, I decided I would like to have the Union flag displayed in the council chamber at our meetings. This simple wish to have our national flag at our meetings had to go to a meeting of the group leaders and the chief executive. Much to my amazement, the outcome of this was that all councillors were circulated, asking them to vote for or against. Much to my amazement, or perhaps not, sadly there were those councillors who voted against it. Thankfully, though, it was carried, which is just as well because had it not been, I had already decided I would go to the media.

The irony is that, each month, the chair presides over a citizenship ceremony to make immigrants from a variety of other countries British citizens. Every ceremony was concluded with each one of the new citizens wishing to be photographed standing next to the Union flag on one side and a photograph of Her Majesty The Queen, may she rest in peace, on the other. At least they respected the Union flag and everything it stands for, even if a number of my fellow councillors did not.

The flag was central to another meeting when my successor took office. At a meeting early on in her year, I noticed that the flag was missing and asked where it had gone. The chair told the meeting that it had been needed somewhere else. I made some enquiries and it seemed that there was no need for the flag elsewhere and that the chair had told the security staff to remove it. The result, eventually, was that she had to apologise to the next full meeting of the council for misleading them. Appalling behaviour!

Public and Charitable Service

I have never played golf, nor was I a great athlete, and pubs were not an attraction to me, so for most of my adult life I have served the public and my community. The thirty-one years as a police officer committed to the public gave me a good service foundation.

When the girls were at primary school, I helped form The Friends of Temple PTA (Temple Street School and Bath Hill School) and became its chairman for a few years. When the girls moved to Oldfield Girls School, in Bath, I joined the PTA there and was vice chairman at one point, and also a parent governor for a period.

In 1980 I was invited to join the Lions Club of Keynsham, and so began a thirty-six-year term of service to Keynsham and Saltford, during which I was president six times, one more presidency than any other member. Sadly, the club has now folded. During my time there, I served as a director for some twenty-eight years. I was also the club PR officer for some twenty-nine years. Beyond the club, I served as zone chairman for a year and another year as deputy district governor.

During my time with the Lions Club, I led two regional appeals, one of which was to raise the money to purchase a mobile retinal screening unit for the Royal United Hospital.

Early on in my service, and as I became president for the first time, I was given a challenge by the zone chairman to coordinate an appeal across clubs to raise money to help return a nurse, Sheryl Skirton, to her homeland in Australia. Sheryl had nursed at

Winford Hospital, which at that time was in North Somerset, and staff there were trying to raise funds to help her. She was married, pregnant and suffering terminal cancer. This, of course, was before the age of emails, and on the very first day, I spent many hours on many phone calls garnering support from many other Lions Clubs in the south-west. The appeal was successful and arrangements had to be made to get Sheryl and her husband to Heathrow. The local private ambulance company, Wings, provided an ambulance, and I accompanied the couple to the airport in another vehicle provided by a member of the Lions Club. Together with her husband, she flew home to Australia, and as the plane touched down she gave birth to her son in the aisle of the plane.

Sheryl had to be hospitalised, and that entailed hospital fees, so I then launched a national appeal and, thanks to national newspaper coverage and radio coverage, we raised a goodly sum for her, but sadly after little more than a week Sheryl passed away. It was a very sad end to her life, but the saving grace was that she had achieved her wish of returning to her native Australia and enabling her son to be born an Australian. Lions Clubs locally could be justifiably proud of their efforts.

During my time with Lions, Jane and I and a couple of others rescued the Keynsham Guide Dogs for the Blind branch from closure, and for five years I chaired the group and met with good levels of success. A dedicated individual called Marcia Cohen had been keeping the branch going on her own. I decided it would be good for the branch to have a president, so I approached the famous children's author Dick King-Smith, who lived in Queen Charlton, just up the road from Keynsham, and he readily agreed. Dick was a lovely gentleman.

Another privileged commitment that came my way during this time was to chair the Avon County Duke of Edinburgh Award Coordinating Committee. This was nice, as it rounded the circle, having successfully achieved my Duke of Edinburgh Gold Award many years earlier. I performed the role of chair for four or five years. Every so often an invitation came to the branch for someone to attend a Garden Party at Buckingham Palace. I had been the chair for only little over a year when such an invitation was received. People on the committee told me that the invitation was normally taken up by the chair. I pointed out that I was very much the new boy on the committee, but I was told it did not matter; I was the chair. So it was that Jane and I had the pleasure of attending a Buckingham Palace Garden Party held to award Duke of Edinburgh Gold Awards to young people. So we were lucky enough to attend Buckingham Palace for a Garden Party on two occasions, and I had also attended with my dad for my Duke of Edinburgh Gold Award presentation.

In May 2011 I was made a Melvin Jones Fellow by Lions Club International, an international award, and on the plaque it read 'Melvin Jones Fellow presented to Alan Hale for Dedicated Humanitarian Services Lions Clubs International Foundation'. I am very proud of that. Melvin Jones was the founder of Lions Clubs International in the middle of the last century.

In 2016, when I became chair of council, I decided I had to leave Lions to afford myself the time to be fully committed to the chairman role.

However, in 2012 I had started the process of founding the Keynsham Foodbank, which opened in 2013 with some eighty volunteers. From the outset and during the Covid crisis of 2019/20 I led them as chairman and project manager, feeding some two thousand people during that Covid period. Sadly, there was a change of trustees and styles were different, and in the age of the 'snowflake' they were upset at a forthright email I had sent to a manager following an incident that needed addressing. Shortly after, two of the new trustees very quickly resigned, one because she did not like the way things were going. When I spoke to the other one and apologised for actually getting him involved, he told me he had left because he did not like the way the trustees were constantly undermining me.

Five managers who had been with the foodbank for many years called a meeting, out of which came a motion of no confidence in the trustees, seeking their resignation within a week. The deadline arrived and they had not offered their resignation. My position became untenable, as did my deputy's position, and we both resigned with heavy hearts. Before the five managers submitted their resignations the trustees wrote to them and sacked them! Sadly, the charity was now being run as though it were a business. For nine years we had been successful, running in a relaxed and low-key way, with no trustees or volunteers seeking remuneration for anything they did, save for buying equipment. Four or five volunteers also left as a result of the situation. It is amazing how such a charitable body can take nine years to come to a wonderfully efficient position, only to be successfully undermined within nine months.

I had also, during the lifetime of the foodbank, founded the Keynsham and Saltford Dementia Action Alliance, and that was going well until the pandemic, when we had to close our main activity, 'Music for the Mind'. It was unfortunate that two of the remaining trustees of the foodbank were also trustees of the Dementia Action Alliance and again I felt it necessary to resign, as I could not see any way of working with them. So for the good of the organisation, I left.

For some twenty years I have been volunteering as a driving examiner for the charity the Institute of Advanced Motorists.

Since about 2004 I have been the volunteer editor of the Keynsham Baptist Church newsletter. This newsletter is published bi-monthly and I have put together over a hundred editions of this twenty-eight-page publication. In 2022 I was also elected as a Deacon of the church.

As I write, I am a Guardian of the British Normandy Memorial and a Governor member of the Royal National Lifeboat Institution. I also volunteer once a week at the National Trust property of Dyrham Park, South Gloucestershire.

At the beginning of 2022 I established Bereavement Support Keynsham and attracted a dozen or more volunteers to provide a monthly drop-in centre for those suffering bereavement. This has proved successful and much needed and recently we added an extra session.

Having had a great life so far, I believe that I have recognised that and reinvested myself in giving back to others within the community, whether that be local or farther afield.

As I tell people, the benefits of being involved in so many things are: one, enjoyment; and two, giving something back for the great life and family I enjoy and love dearly. But the added bonus is that I have no time for decorating, gardening and DIY!

Afterword

I hope that you, the reader, have enjoyed my life up till now half as much as I have, because I feel truly blessed. I have a lovely wife, two lovely daughters, plus my wonderful grandchildren. I have had a great working life, when many have to take what they can get. I have enjoyed my service to the community in its various forms.

May I thank everyone who has played a part in my life, be it large or small; it has all come together to make it a wonderful journey. A journey, I hope, God willing, that will go on for many, many, years yet.

May God bless you all.

Three references for Alan, from Martina Byrne-Obee, Molly Harding and Pam Williams:

Hi Alan,

Hope you and your family are all well.

Wanted to show support to someone who has done everything and more in their power to support me in my different roles within the Road Safety Team.

In fact, without your continuous support and encouragement over the ten years I worked alongside you, I would not be in my current role: Lead Road Safety Officer.

You saw potential and were prepared to take the time to share knowledge and skills to enable me to progress, assisting where required and always happy to listen.

You were non-judgmental of my decisions and encouraged personal development, allowing me to grow within the role, for which I am truly grateful.

Your support as my manager was invaluable, enabling me to be the best I could be within my role.

I hope to see you soon, Alan. Take care and best wishes x

Kind regards

Martina Byrne-Obee
Lead Road Safety Officer

TO WHOM IT MAY CONCERN

Dear Sir or Madam,

I have known Alan for over twenty years and was managed by him for eighteen months around 2001. He was the local Unison branch secretary and I was the administration assistant.

I found him to be a conscientious, reliable, honest and extremely hard-working manager.

He was assertive, passionate about what he did, but would also show compassion and empathy to Union members seeking support. He treated people with respect at every level, but wasn't afraid to ask questions when he thought someone had been treated unfairly. He made sure that everyone felt they had a voice and their opinion would be listened to.

He communicated honestly, which I appreciated, and if he could see a better way of doing something, then he would tell you, but in a supportive and mentoring way. His organisational skills certainly improved the way the Union office was run, particularly around strategic planning and preparation of paperwork for meetings.

Alan was protective of both his staff and volunteers, but would also challenge rudeness or behaviour that potentially could compromise the Union branch. I once left him a pile of papers with a note saying 'Sign these'. The papers were duly signed and put back on my desk with 'please' added to 'Sign these'. Subtle but effective. I always put please after that.

Not only was he considerate of those he managed, but he went above and beyond in protecting them from unfair external criticism. In this regard, he intervened when an individual was unfairly blaming me for something I had not done and stopped the onslaught but in a calm and professional way.

I always found him to be fair and the best manager I have worked under.

Thank you.
Yours sincerely,

Molly Harding

TO WHOM IT MAY CONCERN

22 April 2021

My name is Pamela Williams and this letter is my personal character reference for Alan Hale. I have had the pleasure of knowing Alan Hale since September 2003, when I started working for South Gloucestershire Council and Alan was my direct line manager until he retired in March 2015.

Alan has always shown himself to be an honest, hard-working and conscientious gentleman, always treating people fairly and respectfully. In the time that we worked together Alan managed a team of over fifty people and he was always someone I could rely on for support, encouragement and was a good listener. Alan was an inspirational manager and a wonderful communicator. He had the ability to make a whole room listen and feel engaged with whatever he was saying, no matter what the age group, as he always made it interesting and relevant. He was a wonderful team leader and a true inspiration, he made coming to work a joy and he is a very hard act to follow, as I am now managing the team.

When Alan left in March 2015 it was with great sadness, and to this day I still miss him. We have kept in touch and, although I do not see him on a regular basis, I am pleased to now consider Alan a personal friend.

Yours faithfully,

Pamela Williams
Corsham
Wiltshire

Dear Alan.

Just a note of thanks for the help and encouragement you were to us on the 24th Sept when Dad died at the R.U.H. (MR. M.G Edwards) Thank you very Much for the sensitive way you talked to Mum John & Me + then later Philip too. It was appreciated

Yours gratefully Ruth Peples.

12/11/ao

Dear P.C Hales,

Thank you so much for taking trouble to find my daughter Vanessa Golby & inform her about her father Alan Golby who was dying of a stroke in Royal United Bath Hospital. It made such a difference for Vanessa + for me to be able to say goodbye to Alan before he died.

God bless you

Angela Austin

Lightning Source UK Ltd.
Milton Keynes UK
UKHW051935250223
417660UK00011B/214